The French Immersion Debate

French for All or All for French?

The French Immersion Debate

© 2002 Jeanne-Marie Mannavarayan

National Library of Canada Cataloguing in Publication Data

Mannavarayan, Jeanne-Marie.

The French immersion debate

Includes bibliographical references.

ISBN 1-55059-226-2

1. French language -- Study and teaching as a second language -- Immersion method. I. Title.

PC2065.M36   2001   448'.007   C2001-911523-7

Detselig Enterprises Ltd.

210-1220 Kensington Rd. N.W., Calgary, AB T2N 3P5

Telephone: (403) 283-0900/Fax: (403) 283-6947

E-mail: temeron@telusplanet.net

www.temerondetselig.com

Our website now includes a secure online order form for VISA transactions.

We acknowledge the financial support of the Government of Canada through the Book Publishing Industry Development Program (BPIDP) for our publishing activities.

ISBN: 1-55059-226-2

SAN: 115-0234

Printed in Canada

Acknowledgements

I wish to acknowledge and express appreciation for the guidance and direction of Dr. Diane Dagenais in the preparation of the thesis that gave rise to this book and to recognize the encouragement and assistance of Dr. Kelleen Toohey.

I am most grateful to my students, as well as my own children, for unwittingly being the guiding light that led me to this research and the understanding of the nature of successful learning and how it ties to emotions and motivation. I am indebted to them for providing me with the practical background information without which this study could not have been done.

My appreciation also goes to my husband, Loyolla Mannavarayan, for his untiring support and boundless patience during the challenging years spent at Simon Fraser University. I dedicate this book to him.

Table of Contents

Introduction

In a global economy and increasingly multilingual society, the acquisition of a foreign language has emerged as one of the major goals for children of the next century....Public schools and universities often require their students to demonstrate this competency in foreign language course work prior to graduation....However, this requirement is difficult for many students of average to above-average ability who do not perform well in foreign language courses. (Ganschow, Sparks, Javorsky, 1998, p. 248).

Many years of teaching in the French Immersion and regular French as a second language (FSL) programs have provided time and time again the subject matter that led me to question, analyze and deeply reflect on the suitability of second language programs for all children. Classroom experiences and observations created the first crucial threads of a long and laborious research process that wove itself around a strong desire to understand disturbing episodes, reactions to and results of mediocre language learning. Indeed, it was not hard to concede after so many years in the classroom that schooling in an unfamiliar language had not produced the expected results equally for all. While many students did flourish in this unfamiliar language environment, others appeared to languish, agonize and suffer.

I must specify at this point that I do not equate Immersion bilingualism obtained within the four walls of the classroom to early childhood bilingualism achieved through a natural environment. French Immersion, despite its early emphasis on language learning, remains different from the context of first language development and differs greatly from the informal way in which a child picks up a second language either in the home or in a new social setting.

Both beneficial and harmful consequences of bilingual education are extensively analyzed and discussed in the literature. There is a widespread consensus among researchers that overall, the linguistic and cognitive advantages of bilingualism outweigh its negative effects (if they exist at all). A bilingual education is also said to facilitate the intellectual and neurological development of the learner. These enhanced outcomes are corroborated by research impressively and abundantly reported in the literature (Carringer, 1974; Barik & Swain, 1976; Cummins, 1978; Cummins

& Gulutsan, 1974). Nevertheless, although academic and emotional difficulties exist for only a minority of Immersion students, they are very real and distressing enough to warrant our attention.

My long personal experience of language teaching has brought to light cases inconsistent with the research findings. I have realized over time that some children are adversely affected by bilingual education; they experience learning difficulties, anxiety and discomfort when confronted with the task of learning a language other than their first language. Eventually, I had to reckon with the emergence of my doubt regarding the validity and veracity of the above statements for all students. Over the years, this doubt grew into the shape and form of an imposing question: *Is bilingual education, or French Immersion for that matter, suitable for every child?* I felt that this question, which forms the basis of my inquiry, needed to be addressed.

Some children in French Immersion were indeed experiencing problems. I felt empathy. I could not remain a detached witness, an outside observer or even a sympathetic listener. Gradually, I was drawn inside their experience, wanting desperately to understand it. I do not deny that emotion played an important role in my involvement. In fact, I believe it was the guiding light that eventually led me to the information I was looking for. I began to search and probe the available literature on the subject. I came to realize that the existing research on learning a second language and academic school subjects through the medium of that second language had failed to look at the whole child; it did not appear to take into consideration either the physiological or biological make-up of the learner or her intrinsic personality. Weininger (1982) suggests that "we need more information of a kind resistant to statistical measurements" (p. 33). The information that Weininger has in mind "might give a 'feel' of what happens in intensive early language learning and could usefully complement more rigorously 'scientific' findings and enhance our understanding of what the experience means for the whole child" (p. 33). He adds: "If Immersion is to be evaluated fully as a contribution to early education, we should, I think, be prepared to approach it in terms broader than those which stress academic competencies alone" (p. 34). The "feel" for what is happening to the unhappy students is what concerns me, and my research is an endeavor to fill a void. It is a proposition to examine that aspect of language learning which is neither scientifically measurable, nor always noticeable.

Second language learning, I believe, includes aspects that need to be brought up to the surface and to the public consciousness. It is my conviction that within the field of study of bilingual education, one needs to explore a different kind of information, the kind that could provide some insight into the psycho-emotional state of the learner. This information might indeed lead to a better understanding and a better feel for what goes on when a language learner experiences difficulty. Thus, it is in the field of bilingual education and specifically in the context of the French Immersion programs that I wish to examine and question the suitability of these programs for all children.

This is a qualitative study that challenges the concept of suitability of the French Immersion programs for all children. The ambiguity regarding these programs led me to review the traditional Immersion research field; unfortunately, this research field did not provide any information or explanation that would have permitted me to give meaning to my personal classroom observations. Thus, this book also includes a review of literature on language learning produced in psychology and philosophy, which finally led me to a better and deeper understanding of the same observations.

This research is phenomenological inasmuch as it attempts to describe my perception of my students' experience of a difficult learning situation.[1] It is based on a constructivist epistemology that considers personal experience as a source of knowledge. This research is also a hermeneutic[2] study, as it tries to make sense of what is happening in the classroom to the students with learning difficulties; it strives to interpret the signs of distress and to understand the dynamic and intentionality of the behaviors that some students exhibit in a second language learning situation. Thus, it explores an existential dimension to second language learning that needs to be addressed and understood. The goal is to understand students' personal perspectives and uncover the roots of the problems encountered by considering the "whole child." This in turn helps in sharpening the perception of the students' problems.

This study aims at providing parents, teachers and administrators with a detailed personal observation of the learning difficulties and emotional problems experienced by some children in a second language learning situation.

This book is organized in two parts. In the first part from chapters 1 to 5, I explore the traditional literature on Immersion in search of a better and deeper understanding of some difficult classroom experiences. The rapid growth and success of the Immersion program is seen to contrast drastically with various parental complaints, students' learning difficulties and emotional problems. A significant drop-out rate seems to substantiate and underscore these predicaments. I conclude this section by suggesting an alternative teaching methodology for children experiencing second language difficulties. However, this only partially addresses the above issues.

In the second part of this book, chapters 6 to 9, I review research on Immersion and second language learning that examines influential factors such as IQ, motivation and anxiety – factors which diversely affect the learning process. I also review another body of research outside education literature to argue that it can contribute to our understanding of children's second language learning difficulties. It highlights the physiological and biological limitations associated with such experiences. As well, this literature points to the primary role of emotion in second language learning. Individual experience in language courses is highly complex and constituted by a student's intrapersonal characteristics such as personality, internal dynamics, potential, personal needs and goals.

Chapter I:
Reflections on Some French Immersion Classroom Experiences

This chapter relates my own recollection of the reactions of some of my students, who experienced difficulties in a second language learning situation. These sad cases, encountered during my years as a practicing teacher, form the basis of what prompted me eventually to research the literature on bilingual (and more specifically French Immersion) education.

Observations of Some Immersion Students

The 3 o'clock dismissal bell had just sent a feverish wave of relief through the entire school. My students swiftly packed their books and started to trickle in groups of two or three out the door. Contrasting sharply with their happy mood was Michael's[1] sad and despondent face, which appeared, disappeared and reappeared within the gaps of the ebbing crowd. Finally, they had all gone and he was left sitting at the back of the classroom. A Grade 8 student new to the school, he seemed to favor the last row of desks. As he always arrived at the last minute when all the other seats were taken, he might not have had much choice in sitting in that spot. He had not done the homework for the third consecutive time, this fourth week of September, which consisted of reading a chapter of the assigned novel and of answering the corresponding questions. As I examined him more carefully from my desk, I noticed that he was not reading the opened book on his desk. Instead, he seemed to be staring intensely, glaring even, at some unidentified object beyond the book. He looked absolutely dejected. I remembered how he had previously said he did not understand much of the novel. I suggested the use of a dictionary. He did not respond. Meanwhile, his staring, his motionless demeanor and his deadly silence began to perturb me. I went to sit beside him with the intention of offering help. Suddenly, Michael flung the book and everything else on his desk to the floor. The violent outburst took me by surprise. It sent me into a state of utter confusion. "I hate French, I hate French," he screamed. Then, he buried his face in his arms and began to sob. I quickly and nervously picked up the items from the floor, put them in his bag and tried to pacify him by telling him he did not have to read right now. His sobs continued; they attracted the attention of the custodian, who peeked through the door; I was at a loss to explain the uncomfortable situation. Michael gradually recovered his composure and when he could talk, he explained he could not do the work; it was too hard, he could not understand anything of the novel or the Social Studies textbook. I asked him if he had shared this burden with his parents. He replied that he had and that their answer was that he was lazy and he should try harder. I asked him if he would like me to speak with his parents. "It's no use" he replied swiftly, "They won't listen." Michael sniffled, wiped his red eyes one more time, picked up his bag and left.

With some difficulty, I also recovered my composure and decided to call his parents anyway. His mother was not at all surprised about the after-school episode. She confirmed there was an ongoing battle about the Immersion program, but she and her husband felt that Michael was being stubborn and unco-operative. They wanted him to stay in the program so he would be surrounded by what they believed was a better group of children.

This particular incident disturbed me greatly; I could not set it aside and forget it. Michael was not the first student to declare his dislike for French; but for some reason, he had conveyed it with great impact, so much so, that time and time again the scene of the outburst would flash back in my mind and would start me wondering about other students who did not seem to enjoy learning another language. They were either in the Immersion or the Core French programs. They were currently enrolled students I saw regularly, and past students I remembered vividly.

Gradually, I began to develop an interest in why some students seem to resent second language classes. I pondered at length over some personal past and present classroom experiences of student unhappiness. I tried to make sense of the negative attitudes that varied from downright outward rebellion to stagnant apathy, only to realize they all belonged to a mysterious puzzle that seemed so difficult to solve. Indeed, each case appeared to be the result of a particular set of causes and effects compounded by individual characteristics and experiences. The dynamic of it all would eventually force me to reckon with the intrinsic nature of each student.

In addition to Michael, there was Kevin. He always sat in the front row. He was a very quiet Grade 8 student and seemed lethargic. He always looked tired. He moved slowly; opening books or getting a pen seemed like such strenuous actions. He never complained about anything or raised his hand to ask any question. He never talked, never looked straight at me and hardly ever did any homework. He was also an expert at leaving the classroom unnoticed. Occasionally, I would corner him and request that he sit down and do the work. He would comply and disappear the moment I turned my back. I proposed extra help after school. He also refused the extra help.

On one occasion, at the end of class, I asked him to stay behind because I wanted to talk to him. He sat silently with downcast eyes. He was not answering any of my questions when suddenly he burst into tears. That is when he admitted that he could not understand the French at this level. He said he was not doing any homework because he could not understand any of it and he did not want to open the dictionary for every other word. Besides, the grammar was too difficult and the verb forms too hard to remember. Also, he had not wanted to be in Immersion for the last two years. He added that he was also almost failing English; that did not make any sense to him because, according to the information his mother had been given at the meetings about the benefits of bilingualism, he believed he should be getting smarter. He felt that French bred confusion in his mind and that was the reason he was not doing well in English. I tried to explain that it would be difficult to obtain good grades without doing any work. Nevertheless, all he wanted to do now was to concentrate on his English.

According to him, his parents insisted that he stay in the French immersion program as a means of obtaining a better job later on in life. I called his parents to let them know how he felt. They said they knew all about it and it would not be so bad if he were not so lazy and did not spend so much time socializing with friends. They also wanted him to stay in after school to do extra work as often as necessary.

One day, his mother telephoned the school office and requested an interview. She had finally given in to Kevin's wish to get out of Immersion and wanted to discuss his transfer into the regular English program. The principal, vice-principal, counselor and department head (none of whom had ever taught Kevin) convinced her that this transfer was not in Kevin's best interest; he had invested so many years in the program; he needed to show a stronger commitment by working harder and going for extra help after school.

Kevin did not work harder and never did stay in after school.

He was quick at disappearing at the end of classes. On one occasion, his mother brought him back to school and I had the saddest and most unco-operative adolescent to work with. A month later, Kevin's mother could not take her son's reluctance any more. His marks had dropped further and she demanded his transfer to the regular program.

As well there was Chad, another year, a Grade 9 student who had been in the Immersion program since Kindergarten. He confided to me in the second week of September that he was very sorry that his French was not very good. I replied that everything would be all right with a good effort and attitude. He smiled and remained standing at my desk, head down and hands in his pockets. I thought he looked nervous and asked him if something was bothering him. He said he did not really want to be in the Immersion program, had not wanted to be in it for as long as he could remember and had hoped his parents would have agreed to a transfer this year; unfortunately, they had insisted that he stay in the program and it bothered him immensely.

He hardly attended two French classes in a row. He missed so many classes, he never knew what homework had been assigned or when it was due. His cheeks were a glowing pink, his eyes glistened with intelligence; he looked the picture of health. Yet, he constantly complained about stomach aches. He often called his mother half way through the morning because he was feeling sick and wanted to go home. One day, his mother became impatient and instructed the school secretary to send him back to his class; she would not come to get him until the end of the school day. However, he complained so bitterly about not feeling well that he was allowed to stay in the medical room. He then continued to call home every 15 minutes until finally his mother gave up and came to pick him up. Nevertheless, his doctor could not find anything seriously wrong with him.

Chad did not appear to have any learning disabilities, but his average mark for the course was below 50% later in the term. His father came to see me in the middle of October; he wanted to know how his son could improve his mark, but also let me know that he was quite aware of his son's strong reluctance to be in the French Immersion program. Chad's attendance problem was not new, but it had reached new proportions and was now affecting every area of his school performance. He also related how Chad often fell sick just before leaving for school in the morning and that he was beginning to suspect that his son's ailment was engendered by school unhappiness. At that point it was decided that Chad would get help from his older sister, who had been quite successful in the program. As to Chad's unhappiness and sickly condition, it was hoped that the extra help would lighten the burden and bring a solution to the problem.

In the beginning of December, Chad came to say he was going away to visit his grandmother who lived in the interior of the province. He did not return until the New Year. Upon his return, he tried his best but missed a couple of classes and, by the middle of January, the school counselor explained that Chad was feeling too emotional and nervous about following French classes and that he was transferring immediately into the regular English program. If there was any expectation of an improvement in Chad's attendance pattern and work habits, it was gradually and bitterly crushed over the next few months by Chad's unchanged behavior. The puzzle remains unsolved at this point and I have often wondered if a different, more timely handling of the situation could have led to a happier outcome.

There was Ann, a Grade 11 student, whose mother was francophone. Ann often visited her grand-parents in Quebec. The opportunity of language reinforcement offered by her background unfortunately had not yielded the higher French language performance her parents had hoped for. In fact, Ann's written French was riddled with mistakes and her speech contained more English words than French ones. Very often she did not read assigned chapters of novels and her marks were extremely poor. Many times, she explained she could not read the novel because she did not understand anything. She declined any help. She did not want to be in French Immersion and tried to survive in the program by doing the minimum amount of study and sometimes even less than that, as the homework was often not done. In the past, she had done two extra weeks of work at the end of June in order to secure a pass into Grade 10. In Grade 10, her work habits did not improve. She became more skillful at avoiding the extra help provided during the noon hours. At the end of Grade 10 and two extra weeks of study (a joint decision of parents and the school administration), the same scenario repeated itself.

Her mother came to see me in order to find out how she might help her improve her marks. I found out during our long conversation that Ann hated having to learn French, but that she had no choice on account of her background. Her mother spoke French to her, but Ann invariably answered in English. She also attempted to force Ann to address her in French by ignoring her when she communicated in English; however, this particular stratagem was now poisoning the mother-daughter relationship. In her class speech, Ann would use many English words and francisize many others. Reprimands only brought on bursts of revolt and more flawed language.

Nevertheless, it was decided that Ann would greatly benefit from reading an assigned novel with her mother at home in the hope that her mom's explanations would spare Ann the burden of opening the dictionary so often. For a while, Ann seemed to co-operate and accept her mother's help. Her marks did not improve so much as her attitude that demonstrated a happier disposition, a greater confidence and a more serene demeanor. However, this situation was not to last; her mother came back and announced that the battle of wills had to stop. Ann had only accepted her help for a couple of chapters and was now adamant about leaving the French Immersion program.

The conversation I had with this mother made me realize she was suddenly seeing her daughter's predicament under a different light. She conceded she had been wrong in listening and following the advice of the many well-intentioned educators and administrators she had consulted in the past. She now believed that she should not have forced her daughter to stay in the French Immersion program for so long; instead, she should have recognized and accepted that every one is different and that her daughter's education need not be modeled upon her own wishes – and those of others. She also told me that she had refused another meeting with the principal, vice-principal, counselor and department head, because she now understood the futility of trying to convince her daughter of the importance and usefulness of the Immersion program. She was hoping everyone else would see the situation the way she did.

There was Kate who also left the French Immersion program halfway through Grade 11. She experienced great difficulty with the reading and writing of the language. Every year, she had to spend some extra study time at the end of June in order to be granted a pass into the next grade. Kate had become more sullen than ever and claimed she did not understand anything. She declared at the beginning of the year that her parents had not realized yet how "stupid" she was and that is why they were forcing her to stay in Immersion. These parents had paid for a tutor's help the year before and intended to do so again this year. Kate, who always sat at the back of the class, never seemed to know or to understand what was going on. She had become extremely lethargic, her eyes had that blank look of boredom and the sadness of her face was heartbreaking. She attempted to do the homework at the beginning of the year, but very soon, there was nothing forthcoming. Her mother requested she be assigned a tutor. However, the expected improvement in her work and attitude did not happen.

One day, the tutor contacted me in order to discuss the difficult situation she found herself in. Kate had not wanted to be in Immersion since Grade 8, but her parents had forced her to continue with the program despite increasing difficulties. The tutor found she could not help Kate improve her knowledge of French as Kate had lost interest in French altogether. The extreme passive state she was in did not allow any teaching to bear fruit. The tutor thought that Kate's mental health needed to be taken care of quickly. Suddenly, at the end of January, Kate was transferred into the regular English program.

Then there was Sophia, whom I had never met until the day she appeared in my Grade 9 FSL class. She had been transferred after over 9 years in the French Immersion program. Her parents had been contacted many times in the past regarding her poor performance in the French language. They insisted she would eventually pick up the language and they expected her to graduate with the Immersion certificate. Finally, they had to realize that the situation had become too burdensome for Sophia. They could no longer ignore the poor marks that Sophia was obtaining across the different school subjects, whether they were taught in French or in English. Interestingly enough, Sophia had never given any sign of distress; I was told she had never complained or expressed the wish to be transferred. Anyhow, she tried her best in this very beginner's class she was now following. Yet, although she could communicate and understand simple oral messages, she spoke a broken French and only reached a score of 30% on the written final semester test. The test consisted mostly of blanks to be filled in with different forms of "être" and "avoir," agreements of some adjectives, plurals to be changed into singulars and a few vocabulary words pertaining to close members of the family. She experienced such great confusion about the French language that even at this level she could not achieve success.

There was David, a very jovial Grade 9 boy, always ready to fool around and play jokes on others. He could not sit quietly; he was always looking for distractions and trying to distract others. He loved to attract the teacher's attention and hoped she would not check his homework or ask him to write the test he had missed. However, when asked to come back to complete due homework, he would get irritated or even throw a temper tantrum. Tearing pages from his binder, leaving the classroom and banging the door were common occurrences. He had always experienced great difficulty in expressing himself both orally or in writing. His speech, and he never stopped talking, contained more English than French and one had to know English in order to decipher his written French. His average mark hardly ever reached 35%. This situation had been ongoing for several years. His desperate mother did all that was in her power to encourage and to stimulate him. That meant that no expense was spared in terms of professional help from a qualified native French tutor during both the school year and the summer holidays. This remedial help went on for years. In Grade 10, the tutor and myself communicated and co-operated in order to provide David with the most efficient practice and review, not only of the material taught in class, but also of more simple material he should have mastered in the past. But, David seemed incapable of learning or retaining the most basic grammatical concepts.

His mother said she knew he did not want to be in French Immersion. She could understand his dislike for the subject because he was not an academic student at all. However, his sister had also wanted to transfer into the English program in the past. His sister had given her teachers a rough time, but their mother had not given in and eventually his sister's behavior and work habits had changed for the better. So, David's mother hoped that eventually, she would see the same change happen in David, not realizing somehow that David's personality was very different from his sister's.

In the spring, David was to go away to Saskatchewan to stay with his uncle for two weeks. His mother requested he be given a detailed list of the work he would miss while he was away from school. David came back from his uncle's place with a radiant smile on his face. Those two weeks were "awesome," he said, but naturally, he had done no school work at all. How could he even have given any thought to school? There was so much to do on a farm! Fascinated, I listened to David's tales of chores he accomplished on the farm; he got up so early in the morning, drove the tractor to the fields, fed the animals and milked the cows. He had been on his uncle's farm many times before and now he could not wait until the summer when he would be there again. He just knew he was going to be a farmer. That is what he was meant to be. His friends followed him out hanging on to his words like flies to honey. French? I did not have the heart to mention it again that day.

David failed the year, but he did not care. His mother was forced to reconcile herself to the fact that David did not want to continue in French Immersion and she did not force him to go through the two weeks of extra schoolwork at the end of June. Instead, he flew straight to his uncle's farm on the last day of school.

There were others who "suffered" like David and Chad, Ann, Sophia, and Kate, and Kevin and Michael. And there were others who did not "suffer" so obviously, but whose difficulties must have become too much of a burden at some time; they quietly disappeared from the program. Some would disappear completely from the French department as well. Although they remained in the same school, I never saw Michael or Kevin again. On the other hand, Kate passed by my classroom regularly and in company of friends. Smiling and looking a great deal happier, she would acknowledge me and say hello. I also saw Ann often in the hallways. Surrounded by many friends, she talked and laughed a great deal. Her group was fairly noisy, but that did not stop Ann from waving and saying hello each time we met. One day, Chad ran towards me in the hallway. "It is awesome, it is even scary," he said, "I actually understand my Social Studies book now." As for David, he came back many times to "disturb" my classes. He would suddenly appear at the door and boisterously urge my students to listen carefully and do their homework. Then, with a big smile and a wave of his arm he would say: "See you later."

It seemed obvious that Kate, Ann and David felt happy about the choice they had made. They did not appear to have any resentment. But what had happened to Michael and Kevin? How did they feel after having to put up a fight for getting out of the Immersion program? Were they experiencing greater success in the English program? Or were they simply feeling better about school? Was their dislike of learning a second language simply another aspect of a general underlying dislike for school? Did any of the chronically sick or nervous and emotionally disturbed children ever require the help of a psychologist? All these questions and many more remained unanswered.

These classroom experiences formed the basis of my questioning. I reflected on the fact that the French Immersion program had been praised intensively time and time again. In fact, right from its inception, French Immersion has enjoyed a staggering popularity, with numerous evaluations consistently indicating that children in the program achieve a high degree of second language acquisition without detrimental effects to their English language skills or other academic domains. This unique phenomenon has attracted the attention of many researchers, who have extolled the cognitive advantages of such an education and have confirmed as well the superiority of a bilingual brain (Cummins & Gulutsan, 1974; Barik & Swain, 1976; Cummins, 1978). It has also been deemed suitable and highly recommended for every school age child. On the other hand, my experience with unhappy children, the numerous conversations I had with them, their parents and my colleagues, gradually led me to a different awareness. This valuable information, generated through friendly, honest exchanges during which feelings and opinions were laid bare, kindled my curiosity; it represents the starting point of my questioning and analysis of the suitability of Immersion for all students.

I felt compelled to look for answers, to search for explanations. I needed to understand or at least clarify some aspects of the problems faced by a small number of students in the Immersion program. Had anyone ever addressed them at an individual level? Empathy toward the student's plight might have inspired me to understand and make sense of their problems; for, their body language, their tears, their resistance to tutorial help, their skipping and stomach aches, all created and indicated a real experience of pain. No matter how discerning and reliable my personal and professional observations might have been, I sought to undertake an intensive review of the literature to explain them. The "feel" (Weininger, 1982, p. 33) for what was happening (as explained in the introduction) needed to be supported in a more systematic manner. I had to broaden my vision of the situation in order to complete this personal knowledge; this, in turn, would help me conceptualize the problem.

Like all Immersion teachers, I knew and sincerely believed (as I do today) in the benefits of learning and knowing a second language. Nevertheless, I decided that my investigation into the problems and learning difficulties of some Immersion students should begin with a serious review of the literature, not only on the advantages of a bilingual education in general, but also and in particular, on the advantages of the French Immersion education as we know it in Canada. Somehow, I thought that exploring this traditional literature would also serve to enlighten me on the cause of students' unhappiness and learning difficulties.

Unfortunately, after an extensive and rather disconcerting review of this literature, I felt as if I were trapped in a maze of incomplete and often contradictory evidence, endless debates and unresolved enigma. The literature review only emphasized the gaps and the tensions that exist between the different points of view. Campbell (1992) also expresses disappointment regarding the confusion of this literature:

> *It becomes difficult for the researcher to study problems dispassionately in French Immersion when traditional means of inquiry may be biased. This may be the case in the Canadian context; therefore, it becomes important to listen to practitioners in the field, the French Immersion teachers and administrators, as well as to the children enrolled in the French Immersion program, to gain a greater picture of French Immersion (p. 3). . . . . Possible research bias in favor of French Immersion, coupled with goals and objectives that are open to misinterpretation, leave the program open to many misunderstandings and misinterpretations. (p. 5)*

Then my question about the suitability of Immersion for every child raised many other subsequent questions regarding the learning difficulties and emotional problems of some children in the Immersion program. Questions regarding parents' pressure and expectations, double academic load, traumatic transfer, cognitive ability, motivation, first language skills and second language learning aptitude became part of my research. These additional questions served to highlight the multi-dimensional aspects of the problems. They also exposed a multiplicity of opinions which reinforced the complexity of the situation.

And so I went searching for more information off the beaten path and onto a little trodden one in language learning, that of disciplines like neurobiology, psychology and philosophy. These disciplines were called upon to propose a multi-perspective or multidimensional inter-pretation of the learning difficulties in a second language learning envi-ronment. They provided information that, inferentially, could be applied to the study of the learning difficulties in Immersion; they also provided a wider vision field with which to better examine the concept of suitability of the French Immersion programs for all children.

The literature in these other disciplines provided me with more satis-factory explanations about the learning difficulties and emotional prob-lems of some unhappy and unsuccessful Immersion students. Specifically, this literature provided more detailed information useful to understand-ing what some of my students feel and experience in the Immersion pro-gram. It all gravitated around the emotional functioning of the brain, the intrinsic personality and innate character of such students.

Finally, this research enabled me to propose a new concept of suit-ability of Immersion programs. The literature is strongly re-affirmed by my personal experience of classroom cases which represent a creditable and reliable evidence of reality. Backed up by the literature of other dis-ciplines and drawing on Cummins' (1984) remark: "There is no more reason to expect immersion programs to be the best possible education-al programs for all children than there is to expect regular English pro-grams to be" (p. 82), I would propose that this new concept of suitabil-ity be less inclusive than it has been advocated.

Chapter II:
The Unique Phenomenon

The literature review in this chapter shows the success side of the immersion program – a success underscored by the many cognitive, academic and socio-economic advantages that a bilingual education is known to confer. But if these advantages underlie the reasons why parents enroll their children in the Immersion program, the significant attrition rate leads to the realization that not everyone experiences success or reaps the above-mentioned advantages. This chapter looks at the success of the program and the reasons for switching out of it: the dissatisfaction, the academic difficulties, the need for diversity, remedial help and testing. It also looks at the emotional and behavioral problems students experience in the program.

The Success of French Immersion

In studying the literature on the subject of Immersion, one is dazzled by the remarkable success of this innovative pedagogical practice (Lapkin, Swain & Argue, 1983; Stern, 1984, 1991). The pedagogical practice of *Immersion* consists of teaching all or part of the school subjects through the medium of a language that is not usually spoken at home or in the social environment of the students.

This particular revolutionary method of acquiring a second language has been very popular in Canada for over three decades now. It has had the beneficial and remarkable consequence of fostering a greater public consciousness and understanding of the country's official language duality. Moreover, it has brought forth a new attitude towards language learning and has conveyed to the public that unilingualism can be a disadvantage. This turn-about has been termed by H. Stern (1984) a kind of "quiet language revolution" (p. 506).

Over the years, French Immersion has gained recognition beyond the Canadian borders; in fact, it has enjoyed a world-wide reputation. In the wake of its large success – which demonstrated that it is possible to learn a second language in primary school grades – several other countries were inspired to set up similar language programs. Already in 1984, H. Stern mentions that "Canadian-style immersion experiments are in progress in nineteen American cities" (p. 508). Today, many European countries, Australia as well, are following the Canadian innovation.

The Immersion programs were quite popular and enjoyed a rapid growth (it spread across Canada like a tidal wave). According to M. Stern (1991), the CPF (Canadian Parents for French) Registry of 1990-91 recorded an estimated enrollment of over 102 000 students in the school year 1982-83. It jumped to over 148 000 in 1984-85 (Lewis, 1986) and to over 300 000 in 1996 (Lanmark-Kaye, 1996). In the province of Alberta, in 1988, Hayden also stated that despite a general decline in school population, the number of students enrolled in the French Immersion program was increasing by 600 a year. In Manitoba, the program has also been so successful that, within 12 years, it experienced an increase of 800% (Campbell, 1992). In 1986, Calvé mentioned that the number of students enrolled in the program was five times more than ten years before, and only half the number forecast for the next five years.

In British Columbia alone, the enrollment in French Immersion programs started with a few hundred in the 60s and increased to nearly 19 000 by 1986-87 (Day, Shapson & O'Shea, 1987, p. 1). By 1996, B.C. school districts were offering French Immersion to about 30 000 students (Lanmark-Kaye, 1996).

This unique phenomenon, often referred to as "the great Canadian success story" (Hayden, 1988, p. 223), must be credited in part to the fact that the Immersion program was launched as part of a funded research project (The St. Lambert Experiment) that took place in the 60s and documented the positive results of bilingual education. Since then, many more studies have confirmed the numerous advantages of a bilingual education. Unlike other educational experiments that come and go when research finds that the anticipated effects have not been produced, Immersion results, despite a few controversies, have consistently received favorable reviews, particularly in terms of amount of French learnt at school (H. Stern, 1984). In addition, research indicates that the learning of a second language through French Immersion takes place without undesirable consequences to the cognitive and academic development of the students (Cummins, Gulutsan, 1974; Cummins, 1978). The Immersion program has thus been regarded increasingly as a "highly successful experiment" (Lapkin, Swain & Argue, 1983, p. 5).

It owes its efficacy mainly to the early intensive exposure to the second language.

Advantages of Bilingual Education

French Immersion has been the focus of a great deal of research. Some studies addressed the concern of parents regarding the development of the students' first language (English) and their ability to acquire knowledge in subjects taught in the second language. Many studies reveal that bilingual education and bilingualism enhance the cognitive development of the majority of children. They also document how second language skills progress at no cost to the development of the first language, which remains comparable to that of students educated in a regular English program. As well, research shows that Immersion programs do not result in any subject matter deficit (Cummins, 1978, 1984; Swain, Lapkin, 1982). Moreover, they promote positive attitudes towards the French language and the French culture (Gardner, Lambert, 1972; Cziko, Lambert, Gutter, 1979).

Over 30 years ago, Peal and Lambert (1962) concluded that bilingual children had a verbal and a non-verbal advantage over monolingual children and that their intelligence, concept formation and mental flexibility were favorably affected by their bilingualism. In a more recent past, other researchers reached similar conclusions. They documented higher measures of creativity, conceptual analysis, divergent thinking (Carringer, 1974) and language competence (Barik & Swain, 1976). In fact, Cummins (1978) argues that bilinguals enjoy a neurological, cognitive and academic superiority as well as a more advanced metalinguistic awareness thanks to a more intensive language learning. Intellectually more alert, they benefit from a cognitive flexibility that facilitates the development of a higher degree of originality along with an easier transfer of cognitive abilities to all the other domains of learning (Cummins & Gulutsan, 1974).

Thus, the Early Immersion students[1] are able to apply those skills developed in French to the writing and comprehension of English. They catch up very easily with their peers in an English-only program, and even surpass them sometimes (Barik, Swain, 1978). They do equally well in other subjects like Mathematics, Science or Social Studies (Barik, Swain, 1978).

As for the students of Partial[2] or Late Immersion,[3] they eventually also find themselves on a parity level with English-speaking students of the same age. Moreover, if the English skills of Anglophone children in an Immersion program are not in any way diminished, their understanding of spoken and written French compares favorably with that of average French-speaking students in Quebec by the end of Grade 6. Their productive skills (speaking and writing) though, need some practice through regular contact with native speakers in order to attain the same level of fluency. As publicized by Lapkin, Swain and Argue (1983) in *Immersion: The Trial Balloon That Flew*, the advantages of bilingual education are further enhanced by a greater flexibility in thinking and a better sensitivity to sound and language. Indeed, these children are "blessed with bilingual brains" (p. 15).

Such a rosy picture of bilingual education may lead perforce to the conviction that all children engaged in such a program must naturally outperform their monolingual counterparts in many cognitive and academic tasks. Then, one begins to wonder why some children would want to leave such a valuable pedagogical program and why their parents would allow them to do so.

French Immersion Attrition

However successful the Immersion program is, it is not flawless (Trites & Moretti, 1986). The drop-out rate of the French Immersion program is significantly high. In her Ph.D. thesis, M. Stern (1991) remarks that generally speaking, "while many children are successful in the French Immersion programs and meet their middle class parents' expectations, approximately from 40 to 50% of the children transfer out of the French Immersion program between senior Kindergarten and Grade 6....At the secondary school level, the retention rate is lower, at 20 to 30%" (p. 12).

Students drop out of French Immersion at various levels and very few remain in the program until its conclusion. Past reviews of attrition rates vary according to time and space. According to Trites and Moretti (1986), out of the original 26 children in the pilot French Immersion class of the St. Lambert[4] area of Montreal, only 15 were still in the program by Grade 7. As for the 38 children of the follow-up class, only 25 remained in the program by Grade 6. Adiv (1979) reports an attrition rate of 20% in a Grade 11 student group of Montreal. Halsall (1991), in her summary of the literature review of Canadian secondary level attrition, states that attrition is reported to range from 20 to approximately 80%.

Lewis (1986) reports that in the course of two school years (1984-86), the total overall rate of transfer between Grade 8 and Grade 12 in four districts of British Columbia was 35%, with a high of 54% between Grade 10 and Grade 12. The difference between the rate of transfer for Early Immersion (51.2%) versus Late Immersion (34.5%) was also both significant and interesting. In Winnipeg, one school division registered a loss of over 40% by Grade 9 between the years 1983-1990 (Campbell, 1990). Similar results have been observed in Alberta, where Keep (1993) is concerned with what she calls "the overwhelming problem of attrition" (p. 6). Provincial attrition rates in that province range from 43 to 68% by Grade 6, 58 to 83% by Grade 9 and 88 to 97% by Grade 12 for the period of 1983 to 1991.

One must also mention that following a rapid growth and a steady increase in the number of enrollments, the program reached a plateau in the 90s and appears to be now experiencing a certain decline in popularity. For instance, in the span of seven years (from 1983 to 1990) in the province of Alberta, the enrollment in ECS (Early Childhood Services) showed a growth of 79%. However, since then, a decline of 16% over a two year period (1989-1991), as well as another decline of almost 50% in the Roman Catholic separate school district, point to a reversing trend in enrollment rates. Both the attrition rate and the declining enrollment are part of what Keep (1993) calls an "endemic" (p. 8) situation. This trend is also prevailing in British Columbia, where the district of Coquitlam has seen its total enrollment of 1836 students in 1985 reach a peak of 2720 in 1989, remain fairly steady until 1993 and slowly decrease to a total number of 2235 in 1997. As for the Kindergarten enrollment of the same district, the number of 255 in 1985 increased to 320 in 1989 and fluctuated back and forth and down to 174 in 1997. This represents a drop of over 54%. The Late Immersion enrollment experienced a similar drop from 90 students in 1985 down to 50 in 1997 (District 43, report of January 1998). I would like to mention, though, that some school districts of British Columbia have recently experienced an increase in Immersion enrollment. This has brought the total number of Immersion students from 29 434 to

29 979 – an increase of 0.1% (from 4.8% to 4.9%). However, the percentage of students enrolled in Immersion for the school year 1999/2000 (4.9%) is still lower than the percentage of students enrolled in the program for the year 1989/1990 (5.2%).[5]

Are There Problems?

How can we explain the high attrition rate and some of the present lower enrollments? What is happening to the success story of Canadian Immersion? Is the "trial balloon" slowly deflating? Bibeau (1984) wonders if "the claims made for the success of French Immersion are exaggerated" (p. 44). H. Stern (1982) seems to think that we have been inclined to exaggerate the success of the program: "Much as I like and support Immersion as an exciting and, indeed, essential alternative program in school systems, we do language teaching a disservice by overstating its success and incidentally, also by overlooking its problems" (p. 37).

Numerous researchers, as mentioned previously, have shown that Immersion is a largely successful program in developing second language skills as well as many other academic skills. Yet, parents and students have raised issues that perhaps throw some light on the large number of students who transfer into the regular English program. Webster (1986), a founding member of CPF (Canadian Parents for French), in her article, "Parent Expectations and Reality about Secondary Immersion," asks: "Are there problems?" (p. 10). She can foresee problems with the organization of the Immersion program at the secondary level, in terms of providing enough opportunity to achieve the goal of bilingualism. She wonders if parents were not delivered what they believed was "the unspoken – or spoken – promise?" (p. 10). She is alarmed also by the poor self-assessments of some Grade 12 and 13 Early French Immersion students of the Ottawa and Carlton area (as reported by Pawley in 1985). Their self-assessments, unfortunately, compare quite well with Federal Government evaluations of their skills and ability to cope with French. A Foreign Service Test (also reported by Pawley in 1985) rated them on a scale of 0 to 5 (with possible pluses for each level) and showed that over half of them only received a score of 2 or 2+. What this means in terms of French proficiency, says Webster, is that these students are only able to satisfy limited social and work needs in that language. Another test, the Language Knowledge

Examination, which assesses listening comprehension, speaking, reading and writing abilities, rated as average Immersion students' ability in French. Webster adds: "I believe these results are just not good enough" (p. 10). Lyster (1987) observes that although his Grade 8 students' English skills are not suffering, their receptive listening and reading skills in French are not native-like. They have difficulty understanding films and they struggle with novels intended for young francophones. Their socio-linguistic competence is not well developed either and if they are able to communicate meaning, it is done with little grammatical accuracy. In short, they "speak immersion" (p. 703).

Other researchers also expose the weaknesses of French Immersion. Studying it from different perspectives, they conclude there is not much evidence of progress in the accuracy of spoken French from Grade 2 to Grade 6 and that the gap between correct speech of Francophone pupils and the faulty speech of the Immersion pupils increases over the years (Spilka, 1976). H. Stern (1984) expresses the same idea when he refers to the "ceiling effect that descends on Immersion students after a period of a few years of pleasing steady progress in proficiency" (p. 514). Harley (1984) finds that the poor grammatical skills of the Immersion students are related to their socio-linguistic inadequacies and although they have successfully developed communicative strategies to compensate for their "limited grammatical resources" (p. 60), this, down the line, could turn out to be a hindrance to developing a higher degree of socio-linguistic competence. In fact, Harley remarks that "the socio-linguistic competence of Early Immersion students remain non-native-like into their high school years" (p. 59). Along the same lines, H. Stern (1984) remarks that the students "seem to lack the social and stylistic sense of appropriateness of language use" (p. 514). He further comments that the language spoken by Immersion students remains largely a classroom language devoid of its socio-cultural components. As far as linguistic stagnation is concerned, Bibeau (1984), a specialist on linguistic subjects, examined research conducted by Spilka, Connors and Harley, and concluded that after an initial success in Early Immersion, children "regress in the second language for reasons that seem related to their phase of social identification" (p. 45).[6] Similarly, Hammerly[7] (1989), professor of Applied Linguistics, though criticized by numerous researchers, voiced his personal concerns in very strong terms. He is of the opinion that

"French Immersion results in fairly good listening and reading comprehension (though quite inefficiently). But after 12 or 13 years of Immersion, young people do not speak French but Frenglish, a very incorrect classroom pidgin – a hybrid between limited French vocabulary and almost English structure – and seem to write only slightly better" (p. 20).

Parents hoped to provide a better education by enrolling their children in French Immersion. Shapson (1985) mentions that in British Columbia, 87% of the parents with children enrolled in Immersion wished to see them stay in the program until the end of the secondary level. This is not happening. Are we to interpret the current situation as an indication of disappointment with the program? Did the proponents of French Immersion promise outcomes that perhaps did not materialize, at least for some children?

Reasons for Enrolling in Immersion

Webster (1986), a founding member of CPF, talked of an "unspoken – or spoken – promise" (p. 10) and of parents' expectations regarding the Immersion programs. What were the expected outcomes and what kind of a promise was Webster (1986) referring to? What did parents have in mind when they enrolled their children in the Immersion programs? Was it for a chance at a better education and a unique opportunity at bilingualism? What were their assumptions regarding the learning of the other official language of Canada? Certainly, all the positive and widely publicized reviews of superior academic and cognitive performance of bilingual children appealed to the parents. Perhaps, they became convinced of the worthiness of this new pedagogical approach and surmised it to be the utmost solution to learning French.

Several writers have described the benefits parents expect their children to enjoy in Immersion. In the province of Ontario, Burns and Olson (1981) conducted an investigation on French Immersion programs for the Ontario Institute For Studies in Education (OISE). In their report, they indicate that 97% of the students agree or strongly agree that they are in Immersion because it will give them a better access to jobs and allow them to attain a comfortable socio-economic level. Although 88% of the parents believe that learning a second language is very important and that Immersion, in a bilingual country like Canada, is the best way for their children to become bilingual, they also overtly focus on its inherent promise of a better access to jobs. Similar data are reported by Bonyun, Morrison and Unitt (1986), who find in their Ontario research report that 90% of the parents of students who transferred out of Immersion had chosen the program because of better job prospects for their children.

According to Webster (1986), the expectation is simple: *bilingualism*. However, this term has come to define many degrees of fluency and competency. It is understood though, that Immersion education would lead to functional bilingualism, allowing students to feel comfortable expressing themselves in the second language in all types of situations (school, work, play).

Dube (1993), studying the reasons parents of drop-outs had for originally enrolling their children in the program, finds that they believed it would be easier to learn a second language at an early age and that it was necessary to become bilingual for better opportunities on the job market. One must remember that Canada has been an officially bilingual country since 1968 and that bilingualism has become a requirement for many civil service positions. However, in Dube's study, the bilinguality of Canada and cultural enrichment were not rated nearly so important. In wanting to see their children become bilingual, parents may have been influenced first by the highly publicized beneficial characteristics of bilingual education; Dube (1993) suggests that it is the socio-economic advantages of such an education that appeals to them the most.

Lewis (1986) also finds that among the reasons given by Immersion students for pursuing a bilingual education, better education and job opportunities rated the highest. She is echoed by Lanmark-Kaye (1996), whose analysis of a parent questionnaire leads her to conclude that the main reason for enrolling both gifted and non-gifted children in the Immersion program is that it offers good opportunities and long term benefits. It must be noted as well that expectations regarding the academic and economic advantages of bilingualism seem to be linked to parental feelings of status, prestige and pride (Keep, 1993).

Nevertheless, if the literature has mainly addressed the successful side of the Immersion program, it has left aside many unanswered questions regarding the lack of progress experienced by most drop-outs. It must be emphasized that if indeed there is disappointment with the program, it must emanate mainly from the transfer students who obviously did not find the program suitable in one way or another. On the other hand, despite the fact that some reluctant and unhappy students remain in the program, there are a great number of students who succeed in the French Immersion program. They find the extra work worth the promise of anticipated future socio-economic benefits; they also enjoy the satisfaction and happiness conferred by the knowledge of two languages.

Some studies have attempted to examine the reasons behind the transfers – reasons given by students, parents, teachers, administrators and other professionals.

Reasons for Switching Out of Immersion

Have some parental expectations not been met? Why are so many children switching out of Immersion? Students' unhappiness, parents' disappointment, teachers' poor expertise and qualifications and the content of syllabus have raised concern and questions about the future of the program and led some to look for solutions to the attrition problem.

According to Adiv (1979), the main reasons given for switching out of Immersion are the low marks obtained in courses that are too demanding. Not only are the courses too difficult and lead to failure, but they are not motivating enough to justify investing so much work in them. Their content does not seem to correspond to the future needs of the students, who also begin to fear for their English skills. This very briefly summarizes the litany of complaints that appear fairly regularly in the literature on the reasons for switching out of Immersion. However, no single factor explains or leads to transfer.

Dissatisfaction with the Program

Lewis (1986) reports that students object to the Immersion teachers' high expectations and perceive that success is more easily achieved in the English program; as well, they are not comfortable with the workload and the low marks they obtain in Immersion. Students state that curricular content is limited or irrelevant and course selection is poor. Some students also complain about the quality of instruction and report that the interactions between teacher and students leave much to be desired. Personality conflicts with the Immersion teacher, issues regarding their competency and qualifications, concern about low grades, poor course selection and content, and programming difficulties are also mentioned by Parkin, Morrison and Watkin (1987), Hayden (1988) and Halsall (1991). As well, students complain of not having enough opportunities to use the language in real life situations and of working harder for poorer grades in courses that are boring, demanding, lack variety and are not equivalent to the English ones. Moreover, students report that not being able to keep up is frustrating, as help is not always available in French (Lewis & Shapson, 1989; Halsall, 1991).

Academic Difficulties

All studies dealing with reasons for switching out of Immersion mention academic difficulties as the most important contributing factor in the decision to withdraw from the program. Both French teachers and English teachers report that the inability to concentrate leads to a deficiency in verbal communication and reading skills; most transfer children are in need of extra help in those two areas (Bonyun, Morrison & Unitt, 1986).

Academic difficulties are represented by inabilities to handle academic work, to adjust to reading in another language and in general to cope with the rapid acquisition of language; in turn, these inabilities and the limited capability of the learner to communicate lead to much frustration. All these difficulties are compounded by the inordinate amount of time and effort spent over school work (Day & Shapson, 1983). Parkin, Morrison and Watkin (1987) suggest that major reasons for leaving the Immersion program include a limited ability in understanding and speaking French as well as difficulty in reading in French or English. As well, they indicate that students may experience difficulties in courses like Science or Social Studies where instruction and concepts are given in French. Hayden (1988) relates a parent's concern regarding her child's academic difficulty in Immersion: "If she can't do reading and writing now, she's never going to learn the other school stuff (subjects)" (p. 226). Competency in the language arts is essential for competency in other school subjects. Students find the technical language of Science and Social Studies very difficult to grasp. Frustration builds up as the academic tasks become more and more decontextualized and shift to a more abstract work. A greater precision in language is needed for these tasks. Day and Shapson (1983) relate a parent's comment that conveys what French Immersion became for their child, "a difficult task rather than a learning pleasure" (p. 115). Again, in Day and Shapson (1983), another parent laments: "I feel he has lost a lot by having to concentrate on learning another language" (p. 115). Parents feel there is too much homework that their children are unable to complete without help (help they cannot provide since they possess little or no knowledge of French). Children don't know what to do, do not understand the teacher's expectations and end up disliking school (Hayden, 1988).

Difficulties in trying to master the complexities of the French language are sometimes also expressed in problems with English language skills (Trites & Moretti, 1986; Hayden, 1988; Vedovi, 1992). Dube (1993) reports that difficulty or slow progress with English Language Arts holds a strong third place among the reasons for switching out of Immersion and that those children who transfer, usually experience a lack of success in understanding, reading and speaking French as well.

Comparing the percentages of gifted and non-gifted children who have withdrawn or are considering withdrawing from the program in Grades 4 to 7, Lanmark-Kaye (1996) finds they do not differ significantly. On the other hand, the factors influencing their withdrawal do not follow the same pattern. For the gifted children and their parents, the dissatisfaction with the teacher or the quality of instruction takes precedence over other reasons, like the lack of challenge in the program, boredom and the content deficiencies of the courses offered. For the non-gifted children, again the primary reasons for withdrawing are the difficulties experienced in listening, understanding and communicating in French. Their parents expressed the same views, with as well, a dissatisfaction with the teacher, the quality of instruction and the lack of a support or remedial program to address their children's difficulties.

Need for Diversity and Remedial Help

Both the lack of enrichment and the lack of remedial help needed to overcome program deficiency help boost the rate of attrition (Parkin, Morrison & Watkin, 1987; Hayden, 1988; Lewis, 1986; Keep, 1993; Dube, 1993). Lewis (1986) says:

It has been suggested that the way to attack the dropout problem is to consider what is wrong with the system that fails to meet the needs of a certain group of students instead of concentrating on what is wrong with the students. (p. 50)

It is thought that children with learning difficulties need more individual attention; they should receive extra help from specialists, have access to tapes, follow a slower pace with more emphasis on phonics, spelling and comparisons between the two languages (Dube, 1993, p. 54). Parents and students have much advice to give for improving the program, which in turn could increase the retention rate of students, especially at the secondary level. They "want more courses....up to a complete French program....a wider choice of options....more chances to use French in real situations....exchanges and more exchanges" (Webster, 1986, p. 11). But, "students are not always choosing subjects in French where they are available. Why not?" (p. 11) further wonders Webster. Could it be that the academic subjects of most French courses at the secondary level foster a fear of failure in students who find these subjects difficult? Students at that level also indicate that they need extra time to do well in academic courses. It appears that French courses take up too much of their time and do not permit them to shorten the length of their secondary studies (Halsall, 1991). They also impinge a great deal on their free time. It takes time and effort to learn a second language and perhaps students lack commitment towards bilingualism. However, one could presume that if even the hard task of learning a language has been misconstrued in the minds of parents and students, more students would remain in Immersion if the program were improved. Lewis & Shapson (1989) have proposed a wider range of course options (compulsory or not) to meet the diversity of students' needs. Such courses as Foods, Drama, Media, Journalism, Civilization, Physical Education or Community Recreation are courses students suggested to Lewis (1986). These courses could allow less academic students to use language in a less formal way. In the same vein, students might feel more motivated if they were given more opportunities for viewing films, writing plays and engaging in theatre and restaurant excursions. Lyster (1987) also calls for change; he sees the need for "change in methodology and for specially designed materials for the second language learner which would emphasize accuracy as well as communication" (p. 716).

Undoubtedly, a call for change is in order and as H. Stern (1984) says: "Immersion…is a robust innovation, robust enough to withstand criticism, to allow questioning, to recognize limitations and weaknesses so that it does not decline through complacency, but instead, improves beyond what it can offer at present" (p. 513). Indeed, some Immersion program variations or expansions should be looked into very seriously in response to obvious specific needs and to accommodate the different learning styles of the students. The ultimate goal of serving a wider and more diverse population of students for a greater rate of retention in Immersion may not be economically viable though.

Need for Testing

On the subject of improvement, parents themselves have required a suitable battery of tests which could predict success in Immersion before entering Kindergarten (Parkin, Morrison & Watkin, 1987). Such tests for five year olds, unfortunately, lack reliability. Children change so much at that age that it is very difficult to predict ahead of time whether they possess the characteristics to succeed in Immersion. Those characteristics are not well defined either; no particular variable can guarantee success in the Immersion program. Carroll (1976), author of the *Modern Language Aptitude Test* (MLAT), suggests that it would be almost impossible to devise accurate predictive screening tests for children at this young age. Carroll adds, that at a later stage, levels of linguistic proficiency and accuracy could probably be used as predictors of later achievement in Immersion. Parkin, Morrison and Watkin (1987) emphasize the need for continuous assessment, by both teachers and parents, to determine learning difficulties so as to deal with problems early and effectively. Unfortunately, according to Trites and Moretti (1986), teachers do not seem to be in any better position to predict accurately students' eventual success or failure in the program. In their study of drop-outs and successful children, these authors find that the teachers' rating of readiness for the next grade is not a true indication of future success. They further indicate that teachers seem to apply a great deal more caution "about not advising French immersion than about advising it" (p. 38).

Still, because the switch out of Immersion can negatively impact on the emotional well-being of a child, Wiss (1989) concedes that an early reliable screening capable of recognizing children who might develop problems in bilingual education would be very beneficial: "The challenge is to develop methods and materials that can *differentially* predict success or failure in Immersion as compared with the regular English program" (p. 517). Screening could be used to predict "the interactive effect of the linguistic and academic demands" (p. 527) on children whose difficulties in Immersion could be explained in terms of specific learning disabilities. Those children who are not ready to face the demands of Early Immersion because of some cognitive and linguistic immaturity could start their bilingual education later (in Middle or Late Immersion) and avoid unnecessary failure, frustration and/or loss of self-esteem. Waterston (1990) also recommends "a screening process other than the 'self selection'...path" (p. 43) that parents follow haphazardly.

In any case, parents want to be better informed so they can weigh the advantages and disadvantages in order to form realistic expectations regarding language acquisition and the risks of Immersion education. M. Stern (1991) recommends that parents "be alerted to all the risks and benefits of French Immersion before they can make an informed decision" (p. 248). Parents also want an early identification and notification of the problems experienced by their child in Immersion. They would then be in a better position to amend the situation when problems are discovered (Bonyun, Morrison & Unitt, 1986).

Emotional and Behavioral Problems

Emotional and behavioral problems are other disturbing complaints that are documented in the literature on Immersion. In a personal written communication I received in April 1998, Dr. Trites writes: "We found evidence of negative personality as well as behavioral effects of doing poorly in French immersion and reported these findings in several publications." Bonyun, Morrison and Unitt (1986) also report on students who experience emotional and behavioral difficulties (for a higher proportion of boys than of girls) as well as on difficult relationships with the Immersion teachers. According to these researchers, some children in Immersion have negative attitudes towards school, show reluctance to attend, feel frustrated, withdrawn or lack in confidence and enthusiasm.

While teachers can often observe difficulties very early in the school year, some parents also notice their children's lack of interest. These teachers and parents also report negative effects of the Immersion program on their children in terms of their stalled academic progress and struggle in catching up in the regular English program; they notice a change of attitude for the worst towards the French language; they believe their children's self-image has been damaged by the lack of success (Day & Shapson, 1983). Similar behavioral and social-emotional problems are documented as well by Parkin, Morrison and Watkin (1987) and Trites and Moretti (1986); in fact, they top the list of reasons for switching out of Immersion.

Hayden (1988) thinks that the unhappiness, the frustration and the emotional stress of children are related to the disorientation occasioned by having to cope with the task of understanding another language. Students struggle to make sense of what is said only to feel embarrassment and frustration at not being able to understand the second language. They begin to believe they are not smart. They fall behind academically and they experience a serious reduction in self-confidence. As discomfort sets in, they express sadness about having to attend school, have nightmares, even throw up on the way to school (Dube, 1993). This stressful situation is rather unusual and extreme and it is worth noting that on the contrary, Hayden (1988) thinks that parents of some unsuccessful Immersion children perceive their children as outgoing, having many friends and not disliking school.

As well, Waterston (1990) also finds that, among the reasons cited by parents for switching their children out of Immersion, the most frequently cited are emotional problems. In Kindergarten, children placed in a linguistically foreign environment where they find basic communication next to impossible are bound to feel some emotional upheaval. There are stories of children coming home from school crying (Hammerly, 1989). This reaction may be short-termed, but in some cases, the anxiety and the feeling of insecurity and isolation may last indefinitely.

A much stronger view on the subject of emotional distress is presented by Keep (1993). She observes that although self-esteem, frustration and distress levels could not be measured by a standardized instrument, she is of the opinion that these feelings are felt to a much greater degree by students, parents and teachers facing the learning difficulties in Immersion than by those in similar situations in the English stream.

English teachers in Bonyun, Morrison and Unitt's research (1986) mention the poor self-concept and the sense of failure developed by the transferees as a result of their Immersion experience. Although some of the children have to repeat a grade, the teachers don't feel that the learning difficulties should be attributed to Immersion, but rather to factors like the home situation or simply *learning disabilities*.

The problems and difficulties experienced by many drop-outs bear evidence to the fact that not everyone is successful in Immersion. The numerous testimonies of teachers, parents and psychologists mirror signs of distress very similar to those that appeared in my classroom from time to time: from Michael's emotional outburst and dejected attitude, Chad's anxiety, stomach aches and emotional problems to Kevin's listlessness and academic difficulties; from Ann's frustration to Kate's withdrawal and poor self-esteem. All these students obtained poor results in French as well as in other academic subjects taught in that language. All the characteristics of these children had already been observed, recognized and reported in the literature.

Students seem to experience learning difficulties because they cannot adapt to the linguistic demands of the program one way or another. Reasons and explanations brought forth in the literature are numerous; but are they exhaustive in providing an understanding of these difficulties? I shall examine this question in a later chapter. As well, should the students who experience difficulties persevere in the Immersion program or should they simply be reintegrated into the regular English program? These issues admittedly bring to the forefront the question of the suitability of the Immersion program for every child – a question that the next chapter addresses.

Chapter III:
Suitability of French
Immersion for Every Child

Every parent wants a reassuring answer to the following question: can all children be successful in the program? Burstall (1976) says:

> I asked a leading Canadian researcher what happened to children who fail in an immersion program. He answered, 'Well, none do'. I found this hard to accept because it is very difficult to believe that all children, no matter how high their abilities, or how supportive their parents, would automatically succeed in an immersion program. (p. 212)

Nevertheless, it has become quite clear that not everyone experiences success or satisfaction in the program. Consequently, its efficacy and validity as an educational program suitable for all children is being questioned by some and "researchers are now asking to what extent Immersion programs enrich or inhibit a child's educational development" (Hayden, 1988, p. 222).

The Controversy

As mentioned earlier, some parents request assessment prior to enrolling their children in Immersion. They want reassurance that their child will experience success in the program. Their caution can be understood in light of negative results published by some researchers. For example, as early as 1973, the Neuropsychology Laboratory of the Royal Ottawa Hospital was seeing an increasing number of children from French Immersion programs (Trites & Price, 1976). These children were being referred because of serious school difficulties in spite of average or above average intelligence. They did not show any evidence of emotional disturbance, brain dysfunction or other learning disabilities, like dyslexia. On the other hand, they presented quite a unique neuropsychological profile in terms of a maturational lag in the temporal lobe regions of the brain. (The temporal lobes play an important role in memory as well as verbal and non-verbal perceptual functions; they also contain the auditory centres of the cerebral cortex).

These observations and further studies led Trites and Price (1979) to attempt an early identification of children who would be at risk of failure in a primary French Immersion program. These researchers suggest that a maturational lag, present in some young children, disappears by age nine. They argue that children who suffer from this cerebral developmental delay would not experience success in a primary Immersion program; yet, they might feel quite comfortable in a Late Immersion program when the maturational lag would have resolved itself. Trites' and Price's hypothesis appears to challenge the widespread assumption that the earlier the second language learning starts, the better. It suggests instead that young children may not all benefit by early second language learning. Consequently, it becomes imperative to identify, at an early stage, those at-risk children who would find the additional demands of second language acquisition emotionally and academically harmful; for these children, the primary French Immersion program would not be suitable. On the other hand, these same children can experience success and happiness in the regular English program. Unfortunately, Trites and Moretti (1986) were unable to verify their maturational lag hypothesis, as none of the drop-outs studied chose to enroll in a later Immersion program. The researchers reported that students' earlier unhappy experience seemed to have left them with a permanent negative impression of the program. Moreover, they lacked confidence in their ability to learn French. It appears that their problems had disappeared after transferring to the English stream, whereas the learning disabled children who stayed in Immersion were not faring so well.

A totally different view on the suitability of French Immersion for children with difficulties or disabilities is held by Bruck (1978). She is of the opinion that children with problems in Immersion benefit from their educational experience in several ways: they continue to develop their basic skills and become fairly competent in French. They may exhibit difficulties in reading, spelling or math, but these difficulties are no more serious than those exhibited by children with similar problems in the English stream. In other words, their performance would not differ if they attended the English program. Moreover, they acquire the additional asset of a second language.

Bruck (1978) argues that switching to the English program does not lead to an effective solution as the children continue to suffer from "the same constellation of problems" (p. 886). She adds that switching does not relieve any pressure; instead, it creates emotional distress and damages the child's self-esteem. When a child transfers during or before Grade 3, he finds that the children of the class he is joining are much further ahead with English language skills and so he may have to repeat a grade. Bruck insists that after Grade 3, there is no logical reason to switch a child out of Immersion since he will be getting increased instruction in English and will catch up to his English peers. Bruck (1982) later concludes that there is "no indication of specific interference or deleterious effects caused by two years of instruction in a second language" (p. 57). In short, she maintains that the child's learning process does not suffer from the particular requirements of the second language and the rationale behind switching to the English program, supposedly to lift the burden of difficulties, bears no educational value. Bruck's findings have been cited by many to convey the message that French Immersion is a viable educational program for children with learning disabilities.

Earlier, Genesee (1976) cited studies by Gardner and Lambert (1972), in which they indicated that some of the major factors of successful second language acquisition include motivation and attitude. Therefore, Genesee suggests that all children, not just the intellectually-gifted ones, can master a second language and cope in the French Immersion program. He argues that since the interpersonal communication skills do not depend on measures of IQ, below average students rate as highly as the above average students on all measures of oral production. Thus, Genesee (1976, 1992) recommends the Immersion program for everyone, including below average intelligence students, since they appear to acquire communication skills just as well as the more intelligent students. However, group study and testing can mask individual differences and, as contradictory as it may seem, Genesee (1976) cautiously suggests that "a deeper understanding of individual differences in the cognitive aspects of second language learning would facilitate screening students for French Immersion" (p. 512).

Criticism of Both Positions

Both Bruck's (1982) and Trites' (1986) studies have been criticized on methodological and conceptual grounds (Bernhard, 1993, p. 14). A recurring criticism is that the samples of students and the way the research was conducted do not seem to satisfy the conceptual definition of learning disabilities.

It must be noted that there appears to be little consensus on definitions of learning disabilities. There is, indeed, a great deal of confusion and disagreement surrounding the issue (MacIntyre, Keeton & Agard, 1980). But in spite of this, it is now accepted that some identifiable characteristics of learning disabilities can be recognized as standard; today, many researchers agree on a definition, which along with the clinical syndromes, includes the etiological factor of central nervous system dysfunction (which had been eliminated from previous definitions) (MacIntyre et al., 1980; Beitel, 1986). Bernhard (1993) cites the 1988 definition of the National Joint Committee for Learning Disabilities:

> Learning disabilities *is a generic term that refers to a heterogeneous group of disorders manifested by significant difficulties in the acquisition and use of listening, speaking, reading, writing, reasoning, or mathematical abilities. These disorders are intrinsic to the individual, presumed to be due to central nervous system dysfunction, and may occur across the life span. (p. 3)*

Other earlier definitions included the principle of disparity between performance and predicted potential (MacIntyre et al., 1980).

Critics of Trites' viewpoint claim that, according to the above current construct of learning disabilities, his findings cannot apply to the learning disabled because his subjects had "generally good performance on cognitive, motor and sensory tests" (Bernhard, 1980, p. 5). Moreover, Cummins (1984) argues that the criteria of learning disabilities apply across languages. Therefore, the dysfunctional learning process interfering with the second language would also manifest itself with the first language development of Trites' learning disabled children. Genesee (1983) complains that Trites did not examine the performance of those children who remained in Immersion; consequently, there must be a number of false positives that interfere with the validity of his test as predictor of difficulty in Immersion.

Bruck's diagnosis of language impairment has also been criticized on account of conceptual and methodological grounds. According to Beitel (1986), Bruck's identification process of language impairment did not follow a rigorous procedure. Beitel recomputed all of Bruck's groups' mean scores in terms of mental ages at the time of the diagnosis. Beitel's goal was to obtain "a descriptive specification of the groups' cognitive and linguistic skills as well as an approximate measure of the severity of the disability for each group at the time of the diagnosis" (p. 31). Beitel (1986) found that the experimental groups in Bruck's study did not show a performance low enough in the areas of receptive and expressive language skills to warrant the diagnosis of language impairment (a discrepancy of 12 months below chronological age and nonverbal mental age meets the criteria of severity of disability). Further analyzing Bruck's results, Beitel (1986) suggests that the two English and French "problem" groups were not equal in terms of the severity of their disability. The French Immersion "problem" group had higher scores than the English "problem" group. Beitel concludes that "the evidence does suggest that the two experimental groups may have been experiencing difficulties that were different in nature and it does question the conclusions drawn from their comparison" (p. 51).

Trites and Moretti (1986) also question Bruck's initial diagnosis of language disability. On the basis of the unchanged discrepancy IQ performance of the two experimental French/English groups from Kindergarten to Grade 3, they suggest that the groups "may not have been disabled to the same extent and that the more disabled children did not remain in the French Immersion program to the end of the longitudinal study" (p. 9).

However, despite the fact that Cummins declared in 1979 that "when children encounter difficulties in French Immersion, each case must be judged on its individual merits" (p. 142), the debate continued into the 1980s and until today the two diametrically opposing views have created a great deal of controversy that has not been resolved. Consequently, parents of disabled children and educators are no further ahead about what decision to take on the suitability of the program.

As for me, the controversial findings of the researchers failed to provide the understanding I was looking for. Why did all the remedial help fail to help Kate? Did Sophia not find the double academic load painful? If yes, why did she so complacently accept this demanding load year after year? Did she feel pressured to please her parents? Were Kate and Sophia experiencing specific learning disabilities that would have been present whether they were educated in a unilingual or a bilingual program? Or did the added linguistic component simply accentuate their learning difficulties? Above all, were they going to experience more success now that they had transferred into the regular English program?

Nevertheless, Lyster (1987) is not convinced either that below average students are doing as well as if they were in an English program. As well, Wiss (1989) acknowledges the existence of a subgroup of children predisposed to failure in Early Immersion: "Clinical studies indicate that there may be a subgroup of children for whom Early Immersion programs are not suitable" (p. 518).

Clearly, there is a need to identify Immersion students with learning difficulties. Yet, learning problems are far from identical. They do not present a homogeneous condition and a great variety of syndromes can be found under the classification of a specific disability. In reference to the French Immersion program, this issue is important when it comes to identifying students' specific impairment and associated difficulties (Beitel, 1986). Also very important are the issues of appropriate remedial help in relation to the specific disability if the child is to remain in the program. With a clearer understanding of students' learning disabilities, consequences of switching can also be better evaluated.

Consequences of Transfer

The consequences of transferring students out of French Immersion are a complex and divisive issue for parents, administrators and educators alike; the added apprehensions of creating further discomfort and emotional problems for the students must be considered. Furthermore, guidance about whether or not to transfer a student with difficulties out of Immersion is not provided in the research.

Bruck (1978) claims there are negative consequences to transferring children out of Immersion. She argues that switching out of Immersion is detrimental to children's self-esteem and emotional well-being because their peers would treat them as failures; they would be separated from their friends and would have to re-adjust to a new social environment. However, several studies expose a rather conflicting view on the matter of transferring students with learning difficulties out of Immersion.

According to Bonyun, Morrison and Unitt (1981), about 90% of the parents indicate that after leaving Immersion, their children feel enthusiastic and positive about school; two thirds of the children also show a more positive attitude. Most parents in this study also report that their children's academic progress is going very well or satisfactorily.[1]

In another study, Bonyun, Morrison and Unitt (1986) testify that the transfer process is often seen as being a traumatic experience for students who supposedly see themselves or are seen by their parents as having failed. However, in most transfer cases, these negative effects do not last long and the adjustment takes between less than a week to four months; adjustment at the Kindergarten level happens immediately or within a few days. The change is not traumatic; in fact, it is welcomed as a release from a stressful situation.

Trites and Moretti (1986) do not find any evidence of detrimental effects of dropping out of primary French Immersion programs as a result of learning difficulties, but feel that the early drop-outs, having left an unhappy school situation sooner than the late drop-outs, "appear to be better adjusted personally and socially" (p. 91). On the other hand, these authors do report that long-term follow-up reveals "a mildly negative self-concept amongst the drop-out group in spite of having done well for several years in the English language program....with a specific dislike for French and frequent negative opinions of French immersion programs" (p. 165).

Parkin, Morrison and Watkin (1987) report that not only do most transferees show a significant improvement in academic progress and attitude, but "a lower proportion" of them "than of those classified as low-performing in French or English were in a grade below the expected level" (p. 50). They conclude that little evidence of detrimental effect is observable and that most children adjust well to the change. As for Hayden (1988), she finds in her study that "few (*children*) were unhappy about the switch" (p. 232).

In another study of transfer children, it was found that "the problems in Immersion disappeared in 38% of the cases, decreased in 9.1% of the cases, continued in 9.1% of the cases and in no case did they multiply" (Waterston, 1990, p. 39). Parents in this study "overwhelmingly" (p. 40) feel that they have made the right decision in transferring their child and that the Immersion program is not a suitable program for all children. In their opinion, if the self-esteem of the child is at risk, the disturbance created by the program stands to cause far more damage. Incidentally, it is also reported that the earlier complaints of health problems disappear once the transfer process has taken place; parents say that their children's poor attitudes and behavior problems improve as well (Waterston, 1990). On the subject of transfer consequences, Campbell (1992) also mentions that "In no case studied did it appear that the decision to transfer from the French Immersion program was traumatic for the child" (p. 215).

Thus, it transpires from most studies that when a child is not happy in Immersion, the earlier the switch, the better, as the adjustment time will be negligible if done as early as Kindergarten; children will not have to repeat a grade and will not have to feel like a failure – a feeling which could damage their self-esteem eventually. Bruck's (1979) prognosis of a trauma following a transfer out of Immersion very much surprises me, because it is quite obvious, after so many years as a teacher in the program, that many of the children rather feel a great sense of relief, and if any trauma exists, it is more attributable to the feelings of failure and disappointment that the children's parents and school friends instill in them. Indeed, it is my experience that the children's perception of failure is commensurate to the disappointment they perceive in their parents. Sometimes, parents with high expectations of bilingualism find it difficult to accept the transfer and convey feelings that affect children's self-confidence and esteem.

In her research, Bruck (1985) interprets parents' perception that their children are happier and academically more successful after transfer as an attempt to justify their decision. She also sees in their positive evaluation of the transfer results, the persistence of unresolved conflicts, and in their change of heart about second language learning, a withdrawal of support from the child's bilingual education. Bruck explains this reversal of attitude as a consequence of the transfer. However, it is my personal opinion and experience that parents continue to be very much involved in their children's education after the transfer. They simply come to accept the fact that Immersion is not a suitable program for their children; they do not find it useful for their children's emotional and physical well-being, to persist in a direction that is not bringing the expected results.

Nevertheless, there is little evidence that switching out of Immersion creates trauma or that parents who transfer their children are less committed to bilingualism as an educational option. At the high school level, students transfer because of dissatisfaction and difficulty with courses or because they want to join another special program such as the International Baccalaureate (Lewis, 1986). There does not seem to be any report of negative effects at this level either; students believe, for diverse reasons, that they will be better off in the English stream. At this point, I would like to mention how some verbal exchanges I had with a student brought to light a new perspective on these charges of lower self-esteem and detrimental effects of transfer.

Ann and I were both in the school print room waiting for the availability of the photocopying machine. We started to chat and I took this opportunity to ask her how she was doing in her English classes. I was saddened to hear that Ann was not doing much better than in the past. In fact, she had been failing Math right after switching out of Immersion. She explained that she had found it hard to adapt to the English terminology and had needed tutorial help for a while. She had also experienced some difficult time in English. Her marks at the moment of our conversation were at a failing grade despite the hard work she kept investing into the class. I ventured to ask her if she felt or had felt in the past any regrets about switching out of the Immersion program. She hesitated and then replied that she had mixed feelings about it. On the one hand, she wished she had never been in the program, so she could have applied a more concentrated effort to her English skills; anyway, the change had been a release from a stressful situation. On the other hand, she felt like a "quitter." I remarked that she had put up a very determined fight to obtain her transfer. She said the feeling came from hearing her friends brag about being still in Immersion. Although she loved her friends dearly, she resented them because they were a constant reminder of her past "failure." I found it interesting that these feelings of failure were instilled in her, not by a personal conviction, but rather by what she perceived to be her friends' interpretation of her transfer out of the program.

Soon after this, I met Ann's mother at a school function. She was eager to share her thoughts on her daughter's transfer and present school performance. She more or less echoed what Ann had said about the poor school results. She also said she regretted not allowing Ann to pull out of the Immersion program much sooner than she did. She wished she had listened more seriously and much earlier to her daughter's complaints about experiencing great difficulties with the language. She now believed that the development of Ann's English skills had been thwarted by too long a period in the French Immersion program. Indeed, this was at the root of her present academic difficulties and Ann's potential of success had been greatly diminished by having to struggle with another language. She went on to mention that the transfer had also entailed a social dimension she had not expected; she had been bitterly disappointed by the way the community of Immersion children and parents (her neighbors in particular) had viewed Ann's transfer. For some time Ann was almost ostracized by her friends; it was as if everyone looked upon her as a failure. Nevertheless, Ann was planning now to spend an extra year in school and determined to make it to a college and work her way up to becoming a preschool teacher.

Ann did not feel any trauma or regret about the decision to transfer out Immersion. However, she wished the decision had been taken earlier so she could have finished her secondary education sooner and avoided the unnecessary fights with her mother. She also blamed the program for causing a great deal of hardship and unhappiness at both the educational and social levels.

The Debate Continues

Bruck (1979) deplores the controversy concerning the suitability of Early French Immersion for children with learning problems. As a result, determining the best educational course for the children is left in the hands of parents and educators who make decisions based on their "emotions and intuitions rather than objective facts" (p. 86). "Objective facts" should not and cannot be applied indiscriminately to everyone and anyone. There are individual differences that must be reckoned with. Parents and educators who are close to the problems are not to be dismissed as incompetent judges. As concerned and caring adults, they are better able than standardized tests to interpret a child's deficiencies and lack of school progress. This is not to deny the valuable skills of other professionals in helping to resolve the problem, but parents and teachers, being more familiar with the child's life and school performance, can be of invaluable assistance in trying to make sense of the child's distress signals. The child himself should not be forgotten and should be asked to participate in the evaluation of his particular needs. Emotions and intuitions are not to be rejected as inappropriate and inexpert ways of assessing a situation; they can be trustworthy and accurate sources of cognizance. MacIntyre, Keeton and Agard (1980) concur in claiming that:

Assessment is a human responsibility and not the product of tests.... The results of standardized tests can then be used with the discretion they deserve, tempered with information gathered from other sources and with the professional opinions of the educational needs of the child. (p. 120)

Although French Immersion programs may have been shown repeatedly to be successful for many children, they are not so "effortless" for other children with learning disabilities as Bruck (1979, p. 87) would imply. Bruck advocates the suitability of Immersion even for learning disabled students and the proponents of the program have lent her their full support. Her views are also largely upheld by other researchers like Genesee (1976, 1992) and Cummins (1979). However, judging from parental reports (mentioned above) and from a lengthy personal experience as a teacher in the Immersion program, it is my professional opinion that some children struggle to acquire a very limited competency in French.

The literature on the subject of Immersion shows that researchers have not reached a consensus on the transfer of Immersion students. Some studies refute other studies. Scientifically devised tests have been administered by very qualified researchers (Trites and Bruck) who have reached totally opposite conclusions, and on their trail, other researchers have disagreed and debated to what extent the children who have transferred were learning disabled or with what kind of disabilities they were afflicted. And the subject of transferring Immersion students continues to pre-occupy practitioners and researchers. So far, the research on Immersion has been unable to produce any satisfactory explanation for the learning difficulties of some of the students in the program; and these difficulties cannot be easily discarded as merely representing a dislike for school, as some students display a much happier demeanor once they are transferred out of the program.

The debate continues.

Chapter IV:
Bilingual Education – Caveat

In this chapter I propose to examine divergent views on factors thought to contribute to the second language learning difficulties of some children. I look at the assumptions that underlie the Immersion program and attempt to explain that the Immersion practices, from the early learning start to the communicative approach, although they do lead to a successful experience for most students, can also exert detrimental effects upon others. A further exploration of the traditional literature on Immersion reveals that the methodological practice of the program can thwart the linguistic progress of the weaker students and result in emotional trauma.

Disadvantages of Bilingual Education

Much has been said about the advantages of bilingual education and all the academic cognitive and neurological benefits that could be reaped from it. The Immersion program has been praised in many ways for engendering favorable outcomes and not producing undesirable consequences. Its success is such that it has been called the "Canadian credo of second language learning" (H. Stern, 1982, p. 37). Yet, researchers were not always convinced of the existence of a link between intellectual development and bilinguality. In the past, bilingualism was believed to be harmful and detrimental to the academic and linguistic development of the person. Pintner and Keller (1922) reported that bilinguals showed evidence of a linguistic handicap. Saer (1923) mentioned the existence of "mental confusion" (p. 38) in individuals subjected to two linguistic codes in their environment. Macnamara (1966) also found that bilingualism produced adverse effects on the cognitive and psychological development of learners. They exhibited a kind of verbal linguistic "retardation" (p. 37). This retardation, he explained, was due to a "balance effect" (p. 15) – the result of a diminishing competence in the first language, correlated to an increasing competence in the second language. A bilingual person would thus be a disadvantaged speaker in both languages. More recently, the research in Sweden of Skutnabb-Kangas and Toukomaa (1976) has advanced a similar construct. The low linguistic abilities displayed in both languages by the young Finnish migrants in Sweden have been described as a "semi-lingualism," which is a term they use to refer to the detrimental effects of a school system that promotes second language learning at the expense of first language development.

Such reports of negative effects of bilingual education can be explained in terms of socio-economic status, majority/minority language and additive/subtractive bilingualism. The bilingual children of the studies showing negative outcomes, such as those quoted by Skutnabb-Kangas and Toukomaa (1976), relate to minority children: they belong to an ethnolinguistic minority and speak a language other than the one recognized as the official language of the country they live in. This official language, culturally and economically more prestigious than their own, threatens their identity. They are developing what Lambert (1974) calls a subtractive form of bilingualism, which leads to an inferior level of language acquisition for both the first and second languages. On the other hand, the bilingual children of successful Immersion programs such as French Immersion are majority children: they speak the official language of the country they live in and consequently do not feel threatened in their socio-linguistic identity by learning another language. They are in an additive situation of bilingualism (Lambert, 1974) which results in a higher level of first and second language learning.

So research shows that we should not fear for our French Immersion students. They belong to an English majority language group and should not suffer any of the negative effects that minority language children are said to experience. We can be quite confident that the program will not turn out semi-linguals.[1]

Still, some children in the program experience emotional problems as well as academic difficulties (according to Lewis [1986], 57% of transferred students had difficulty with the courses). In view of this, the proclaimed beneficial outcomes of bilingual education become a paradoxical and contentious issue; it raises serious concerns regarding the pedagogical practice of the French Immersion program and the possible negative outcomes it might yield for some students.

Even if the end product of the program is not equilingualism or balanced bilingualism for all (which is hard to attain for most people anyway), does the Immersion program really help the cognitive development of high and low IQ students alike or does it affect the latter adversely? Perhaps, a review of what the program assumes regarding the language learning process within the four walls of the classroom will help to elucidate this dilemma and augment our understanding of what is ailing some children in the Immersion program.

Assumptions Underlying the Immersion Program

The Earlier the Better

An assumption of the Immersion program is that the earlier the second language learning starts, the better. However, there are advantages inherent to all ages. Research has shown there is no "critical" period or "optimal" age for the efficient learning of a second language (Bogaards, 1991). An early start in language learning does not guarantee acquisition except perhaps in a natural environment where very young children, thanks to their cerebral plasticity and their physiological flexibility, are able to reproduce authentically the pronunciation of the target language. In fact:

> *There are so many factors (cognitive, affective and neurological) that enter into the acquisition of a second language; there are so many aspects of language (pronunciation, grammar, vocabulary) that are favored by different age groups that it is clearly impossible to speak of one optimal age. No one age emerges as critical. (Moeller, 1988, p. 11)*

Older learners enjoy a greater development of their mother tongue and generally possess a higher level of meta-linguistic awareness and a more advanced competency in developing learning strategies. They also display more sophistication in the use of rational thinking that permits comparative analysis of the two languages and enables them to attend to self correction. On the other hand, very young learners lack the cognitive maturity that a focus on grammar requires in order to produce accurate output in the target language. Therefore, in the artificial classroom environment, perhaps, some of these very young learners find themselves in great difficulty because they lack the cognitive development or the meta-linguistic awareness necessary to make sense of the scarce immediate feedback of the teacher. Weininger (1982) writes:

> Except in 'optimal circumstances' associated with socio-economic sta-
> tus, confidence about the mother tongue, committed parental support,
> and opportunities to use the new language outside the classroom, I sus-
> pect that the kind of 'head start' which Immersion provides might well
> be making demands that distort rather than enrich the child's experi-
> ence in a period of rapid and complex natural development. (p. 34)

I suspect that the students with initial learning difficulties might
benefit from a later start (in Middle or Late Immersion) as opposed to
an earlier start (in Early Immersion) when their cognitive maturity has
reached a higher level of functioning and they are then able to compare
and contrast the organization of the two languages. Children who can
consciously and explicitly engage in the practice of contrastive analysis
and become aware of the similarities and differences of the two languages can also greatly increase their potential chances of attaining a
higher level of language competency.

A By-product of Other Pursuits

Another assumption of the French Immersion program is that a language is best learned as a "by-product of other pursuits" (Stern, Swain,
McLean, 1976, p. 100) through a communication experience and
worthwhile activities. The rationale behind the French Immersion program is that the learning of a second language is more effective when
used as a teaching medium that conveys meaningful content. Carey
(1984) describes the Immersion methodology as follows:

> The methodology employed in Immersion programs begins with an
> emphasis on the naturalistic and communicative functions of language
> acquisition in a contextually embedded environment, where the
> emphasis is on the comprehension and production of language, with a
> greater emphasis on communicative function than on form. Gradually,
> vocabulary is acquired in context, and grammar is taught through a
> method encouraging more effective communication rather than as
> abstract rules for producing structures. Similarly, through the student-
> teacher interaction, implicit correction by the teacher is performed in
> a manner similar to that in a naturalistic environment, although
> grammar is taught more formally as the student progresses. (p. 254)

A Comprehensible Input

Cummins (1983), in a CPF special report, declares that "the Immersion experience is designed to mimic the process through which children learned their first language" (Research Findings from French Immersion Programs Across Canada: A Parent's Guide, p. 3).

Krashen[2] (1984) recognizes in Immersion "the most successful programme ever recorded in the professional language teaching literature" (p. 61) and views its success as an important contribution to "the solution of some very serious problems in language teaching" (p. 61). He attributes this great success to second language theory, whereby we acquire language "in only one way: when we understand messages in that language, when we receive comprehensible input" (p. 61). He further explains that "Immersion programmes succeed in teaching the second language because...they provide students with a great deal of comprehensible input" and "the focus is on the message and not the form, on *what* is being said rather than *how* it is said" (p. 62). Although the Immersion program did not evolve from the implementation of Krashen's theory, according to Swain and Lapkin (1986), Krashen's theory by which "learners acquire grammatical structure by understanding messages – by 'going for meaning' rather than by focusing on form...by hearing comprehensible input...certainly reflects the language learning context of Immersion students" (p. 6). It is easily assumed then, that French Immersion students acquire the second language incidentally thanks to the communicative pedagogy of the program. It is also expected that as long as the students communicate, they will implicitly acquire the right forms of the language. However, according to Lyster's (1987) experience as an Immersion teacher, students are not surrounded by second-language speakers and the classroom learning set-up does not duplicate the natural environment. Students are not acquiring French in the same way they acquired their mother tongue, for they are not *immersed* among native speakers of the target language. The teacher is the only provider of accurate, comprehensible input in that language – an input that "does not permeate the environment beyond the classroom" says Lyster (1987, p. 705). Consequently, it becomes very difficult for the students who experience learning problems to acquire the correct form of the language, especially since demands for output in form of communication, exceed the available input (Lyster, 1987). Moreover, the students are exposed to material designed for native speakers, and the difficult contents of this material exert undue pressure and anxiety and represent a great deal of incomprehensible input for those children with learning difficulties.

A Reciprocal Interaction

When dealing with learning difficulties, the general pedagogical assumptions in the past have been that students need to be provided with task analysis, sequential learning and instruction proceeding from simpler to more complex tasks:

> *This process requires that concepts be broken into task components, which are then broken into skills. Finally, steps are outlined to help the student master each skill. By following this procedure, the teacher can develop a list of skills which, when mastered, will yield a successfully completed task. In turn, as several tasks are learned, concepts will be mastered....Once the component steps of a task have been identified, the child is presented with each sequential task until a task is presented that the child can perform without error [Wallace & Kauffman,[3] 1981]. Following an analysis of the pupil's errors, the teacher usually designs a remedial program based on the same sequence of skills as in the task-analysis process. (Plata,[4] 1982: 26-27)[5]*

Cummins (1984) calls this type of graded teaching a "transmission" model of teaching (p. 223). (The terminology is borrowed from Barnes[6] [1976]). This transmission model of teaching, according to Cummins "contravenes what we know about how language and thinking skills are acquired by young children" and could be "a potential cause or contributor to children's learning difficulties" (p. 223). Cummins (1984) proposes instead a "reciprocal interaction" model of pedagogy (p. 224) which emphasizes, among other recommendations, "genuine dialogue between student and teacher, and guidance and facilitation rather than control of student learning by the teacher" (p. 224). Cummins (1984) is of the opinion that the "transmission" model of classroom teaching does not resemble the home adult-child linguistic interaction:

> *In the transmission oriented classrooms...the children's involvement in the learning process is largely confined to passive reception of prese-quenced knowledge and skills. Children tend to become focused on the correctness of formal surface features of language and their motivation to carry out academic tasks is largely extrinsic. (p. 230)*

By contrast, Cummins advocates an active use of language in an interactional environment so children can become "intrinsically involved and personally committed to completion of challenging academic activities" (p. 230). These principles underlie the meaningful practice of the second language with target language speakers. The interaction provides the valuable "comprehensible input" (p. 231) endorsed by Krashen (1982). This "comprehensible input" is thus generated by meaningful communication which represents the central function of language.

To illustrate his pedagogical recommendations, Cummins (1984) compares the Immersion and the Core French programs. He contrasts the "impressive language acquisition" (p. 232) of the French Immersion students to the "dismal failure" (p. 232) of their traditional French programs counterparts. The successful result of the former is attributed to a teacher/student meaningful interaction, embedded in a comprehensible input that bears similarities to first language acquisition. The failure of the latter is attributed to the use of pattern drills that do not allow for reciprocal interaction between teacher and student.

I would suggest that the comparison does not stand on fair grounds. The Immersion students have accumulated roughly 7000 hours of instruction by the time they graduate, whereas by the same time, the traditional French program students have only received about 400 hours of instruction. Calvé (1983) wonders if we should weigh the Immersion success in terms of time investment rather than in terms of pedagogy:

> It would be interesting to know if, for instance, in Immersion it is really the language's being taught in a 'functional' setting that gives it the advantage over the core programs, or if it is not rather the thousands of hours of exposure to the language that makes the difference [plus the higher IQs, the greater motivation]. (p. 50)

Nevertheless, in a research project that compares B.C. school Grade 11 Early Immersion students and Grade 11 Core French students, Tatto (1983) found that both groups, although different in their sound discrimination skills,[7] tended to make a similar number and type of errors in their written productions. Tatto (1983) adds: "Neither group displayed a firm command of French grammar. Many non-native-like writing characteristics were observed in both groups" (p. 49). Tatto

(1983) explains:

> *It appears that although the FI students were exposed to French in the early grades, they continue to rely on English because...[among other reasons] contact with French speaking peers is very limited...these students live in an English-speaking environment which does not provide adequate opportunity to use French in real acts of communication. (p. 56)*

This last statement raises the issue of language learning environment. The Immersion classroom hardly reproduces the characteristics of natural language development. Weininger (1982) states: "It is nevertheless clear that the Immersion classroom, in the context of natural mother-tongue development, differs not only from the patient, flexible and affectionate home but also from the informal setting in which children 'pick up' a second language" (p. 31). So, it appears that the "reciprocal interaction" model of pedagogy proclaimed by Cummins (1984, p. 224) may not be such an easy pedagogical practice to implement after all. On one hand, the transmission model of classroom teaching does not resemble the adult-child linguistic interaction, and on the other hand, how many times a day and with how many of the students can a "genuine dialogue between students and teacher" (p. 224) occur? How many target language speakers, providers of "comprehensible input" (other than the teacher) are present in the classroom? A reciprocal interaction may help students develop fluency, but accuracy is missing. Swain and Lapkin (1986), in their review of studies carried out on Immersion students' French proficiency, point out that "from a diagnostic perspective, grammatical weaknesses appear the most problematic" (p. 6). They claim that the input of the teacher in Immersion is too limited for the students to acquire the desired accuracy. They propose instead to have the students produce more written or spoken output and to interact more often with other learners and target language speakers. They then argue that more grammar drills are not the answer[8] to a better acquisition of a native-speaker competence and that it is through the mini language lessons provided by more opportunities to hear and use French that the Immersion students will resolve the problem of grammatical weaknesses in their speech. However, Lyster (1987) thinks that this practice of a high degree of interaction between students only helps students develop more fluency but still no accuracy. In fact, according to Lyster (1987), they develop an output that is "riddled with anglicisms and persistent errors" (p. 703). Interestingly, Heesoon

(1982) finds that:

> *Excellent linguistic instruction, the opportunity to use the second language with its speakers, and motivation are not as significant as the target language speakers paying individual attention to the second-language learner. (p. 87)....The opportunity to practice language is not important in predicting oral proficiency as measured by a formal test. Rather, the opportunity to be addressed by the target language speakers is a crucial factor in determining formal oral proficiency. (p. 88)*

Anyhow, one cannot deny that the success of the Immersion program has been impressive; however, I wonder if this success is not merely due to the fact that the graduating students were able to adapt to and thrive on the communicative and meaningful interaction that the program practices. As for the learning "disabled" students, naturally with greater exposure to the language, they acquire more knowledge of French in an Immersion program than they would in a traditional program. However, are we to surmise that the "potential advantages" (Cummins, 1984, p. 176) of this situation take precedence over the unhappiness and the learning difficulties some of these children experience? A closer examination of the program may enlighten us on what conceivably contributes to some of the Immersion students' poor linguistic results as well as to their psychological and emotional correlates.

A Damaging Experience for Some?

Interlanguage and Fossilization

Stern, Lapkin and McLean (1976) suggest that perhaps informal learning through communication may not be enough, as this practice may lead to a special interlanguage[9] they call "an Immersion class dialect" (p. 101). This interlanguage does not always undergo the expected progress as the years go by. The students are still quite capable of producing "comprehensible" output since they manage to make themselves intelligible, but this output evidently lacks accuracy (Harley, 1984; Lapkin, Swain, 1984; Bibeau, 1984; Hammerly, 1989).

Harley and Swain (1978) also suggest that "Once the children have reached a point in their language development where they can make themselves understood to their teacher and classmates [as they clearly have], there is no strong social incentive to develop further towards native speaker norms" (p. 38). On the same subject, Calvé (1986) remarks that students who are congratulated for successfully getting the message across, however ungrammatically, end up feeling very satisfied with their faulty speech. Such classroom practices breed leniency towards mistakes and tend to encourage a lack of effort towards achieving correctness and precision of language.

Paradoxically, Lapkin and Swain (1984) state in their reports of French Immersion students' language assessment that the students' skills reach near native competency. Indeed, the very young children may appear quite fluent and uninhibited in expressing themselves in the second language. However, in 1989, Lapkin and Swain seem to have adopted a very different opinion: "the French spoken (and written) by the immersion students is, in many ways non native-like" (p. 153).

Genesee et al. (1985) suggest that "there may be an upper limit to second-language proficiency that can be achieved in a school context that does not include a substantial opportunity for peer interaction in the second language" (p. 684). Linguistic accuracy cannot take care of itself, mistakes eventually resist change and a persistent recourse to the mother tongue structures leads to what Lyster (1987) calls "negative transfer" (p. 706). The interlanguage thus created eventually reaches a ceiling often referred to as language fossilization (Lyster, 1987; Calvé, 1986).

The stronger students who seem to function quite normally or even thrive in the different and less structured linguistic environment may not feel affected at all in their comprehension of school subjects. In fact, they invariably prove they can perform equally well in the receptive and the productive aspects of the language and they eventually succeed in attaining a fairly high level of competency and fluency. On the other hand, students with learning difficulties might suffer and languish in a language learning situation that might not be quite adapted to their needs. These students may appear to speak the second language well enough to be understood in a contextually embedded environment, but they quickly encounter difficulty with decontextualized reading and writing tasks, mainly because of their fossilized interlanguage. The latter, in turn, would impede greatly the development of linguistic fluency and accuracy. When these students are forced to express themselves, they can only do it in a very awkward manner.

Psychological and Emotional Effects

Students' reactions to these learning circumstances can be diverse and varied and of a deep nature. The feeling of discomfort leads to frustrations, inhibition and eventually negative attitudes. Indeed, in some cases students feel traumatized by such a situation (Bouton, 1974, p. 173). The acquisition of a second language is based upon previously established verbal habits specific to the native language. The verbal output of the second language is thus influenced by the filter of the native language. A strong first language filter does not permit the weak students to access directly the content of the second language message. They cannot tackle the difficulty; they become partially or completely introverted and apathetic; the learning constraints are such that they adopt a refusal attitude or give up altogether (Bouton, 1974, p. 226).

Skepticism has been expressed by some educators and psychologists alike regarding the beneficial effects of Immersion. Stern, Swain and McLean (1976) report that there is a strong disagreement regarding the constant exposure to a second language in the classroom. They further report that a number of educators and psychologists claim that this second language must impede the child's free expression and create negative psychological effects leading to the development of future mental health problems and that of an alienated disposition in adolescence. Stern, Swain and McLean (1976) also expose some of the accusations the Immersion program has had to face and defend itself against: "Immersion, it is claimed, can be disorienting, emotionally damaging, and intellectually stultifying" (p. 45). These are grave accusations, but according to Stern, Swain and McLean (1976) and Halpern, Martin and Kirby (1976), research results bear no evidence to support these accusations. In fact, they report that numerous studies of Immersion programs (already mentioned earlier) have all found that the children learn without undesirable consequences and that there is no evidence of detrimental effect either on their personality or their psychological and social development.

Nevertheless, the long-term effects of Immersion might not be apparent in one or two year long studies. As well, despite reports of average normal development with no serious deficits for children with difficulties in Immersion, some individuals' deficits may not be readily apparent. I have witnessed that under such circumstances as schooling in an unfamiliar language, children with learning difficulties can and do experience poor linguistic results eventually. Understandably, these poor linguistic results can also lead to further emotional and socio-psychological difficulties later on. According to Barbara Bresver (2000),[10] a Toronto-based psychologist, French Immersion has done more harm than good for many children. Nevertheless, a time has come to advance some tentative suggestions for a remedial teaching methodology which might help second language students with difficulties to avert an unhappy learning experience; for above all, a second language learning experience should remain comfortable and enjoyable enough so weaker students can still reap the benefits of bi-literacy skills.

Chapter V:
A Case for a New
Teaching Methodology

This chapter presents some teaching suggestions by educators and psychologists interested in second language learning difficulties. In light of the assumptions underlying the Immersion program (in the previous chapter), I would like to bring up the subject of the students' level of potential performance. According to the Vygotskyan theory of learning, the level of potential performance is very important; not only should it be taken into consideration when seeking to recognize learning problems but it is also very valuable when offering individual remedial help.

A New Linguistic Syllabus

I would suggest that the poor progress of children with learning difficulties in Immersion further interferes with their reading comprehension of textbooks as well as with their oral and written expression. Lyster (1987) suggests that in order to avoid early fossilization:

> We need to develop a new linguistic syllabus for French Immersion which would combine the program's truly communicative aspects with a more systematic and graded language component aimed at second-language learners. This français component should follow a progression beginning in the lower grades in order to avoid early fossilization, and its content could be influenced by a contrastive analysis in an attempt to counteract the overwhelming influence of English. (p. 705)

Lyster's proposal might be a viable teaching methodology that could help weaker students develop better comprehension and better production skills in the target language. Lyster recommends the use of specially designed materials to emphasize accuracy and communication, and also teaching procedures such as "drill work and error correction focusing on grammatical or functional aspects presented sequentially and then exploited communicatively in context" (p. 715). These pedagogical measures might help ease or even avoid the linguistic confusion of the children struggling in Immersion. A similar intervention is also recommended by Levine (1987):

> *Often there is a need for highly specific drill in mastering the gram-*
> *matical rules of a language. Many students with learning problems*
> *have a tendency to gloss over such regularities. As the complexity of spo-*
> *ken and written material increases during the year, their lack of a true,*
> *basic understanding of the structure of a foreign language catches up*
> *with them. For this reason, fundamentals – word order, morphology,*
> *and syntax – need to be constantly emphasized. This return to basics*
> *has to be the cornerstone of remedial help for floundering language*
> *learners. (p. 380)*

Yet, in his research of a few cases of learning disabled adults who
experienced extreme difficulties in a foreign language classroom,
Mabbott (1994) finds that: "All of the subjects had very strong ideas
about how foreign language should be taught to help them succeed, and
they agreed that it should be done orally in a communicative context,
rather than be focused on grammar" (p. 311). However, it must be mentioned that Mabbott's subjects obtained their high degree of fluency outside the classroom in real immersion settings "as foreign exchange students, by marrying a native speaker, by working with migrant laborers"
(p. 293). The classroom cannot possibly reproduce such *opportunities*!

Lyster (1987) also emphasizes the usefulness of contrastive analysis:

> *Efficient second-language teaching should aim to make the learner's*
> *mother tongue a facilitating factor in the learning process rather than*
> *an interfering factor…students should be encouraged to develop strate-*
> *gies to distinguish between positive and negative transfer. In this way,*
> *contrastive analysis can effectively contribute to the development of a*
> *linguistic syllabus. However, contrastive analysis can only offer a lim-*
> *ited view of the L2 learning process, and must be combined with error*
> *analysis…(p. 715)*

He is echoed by Levine (1987), who stresses that language teaching
"should be based on an understanding of differences between the new
language and English and on an awareness of common roots. The *logic*
of the foreign language should be stressed as much as possible" (p. 380).

Stern, Lapkin and McLean (1976) also suggest that some formal
teaching of French in the form of deliberate language practice and drills
might not be entirely out of place in an Immersion program. Calvé
(1986) reflects as well on the necessity of keeping a balance between the

systematic study of the linguistic code and the practice of communication. He also emphasizes that explicit grammar rules and systematic exercises play an important role in language teaching/learning.[1] Along the same line, Lapkin and Carroll (1988) also suggest that inter-linguistic teaching techniques integrating both first and second language might support the development of vocabulary. They also concur with both Lyster and Calvé in recognizing the benefits of teaching practices that attract students' attention to linguistic aspects of the two languages in an *"explicit and systematic"* way (p. 37) (my translation). Lapkin and Swain (1989) stress that what is needed by the "non-native-like" (p. 153) Immersion students is a "carefully planned *integration* of language and content" (p. 153) teaching. As for Sparks, Ganschow et al. (1992), they recommend instruction "with an emphasis on 'cracking the code'" (p. 48) of the new language through a multi-sensory structured approach.

This view of language learning[2] may clash with Krashen's (1984) principles of second language acquisition (going for meaning rather than focusing on form), and with Cummins' (1984) "reciprocal interaction" model of pedagogy, but one must remember that comparisons of language teaching methodologies (let us recall that we are dealing with *classroom* language learning) have failed to demonstrate the superiority of one method over another. Already in 1899, Sweet[3] observed: "until every one recognizes that there is no royal road to languages…the public will continue to run after one new method after the other, only to return disappointed to the old routine" (p. viii). Skehan (1991) notes: "It seems clear that a possible reason for the failure [of one method over another] to find significant effects is that such studies lump all learners together" (p. 295). Learners present different characteristics and language instruction should take this into account and adapt accordingly to become more efficient:

> *Researchers have attempted to identify the general [and even unique] 'best methodology' or best approach to teaching with less attention being paid to constraints on the operation of [say] methodology or on the way it may affect some people in different ways. (Skehan, 1991, p. 276)*

Success for some learners could then be a question of matching them with the appropriate instructional conditions.

On the subject of teaching a foreign language to students with foreign language learning problems, Ganschow, Sparks and Javorsky (1998) report that:

> *In the last decade…most FL educators have advocated teaching a foreign language through 'natural communication' approaches to learning, which emphasize the contextual and meaning aspects of FL learning and de-emphasize the teaching of the sound, sound-symbol, and grammatical rules systems. (p. 253)*

They continue to say that:

> *FL educators have not generated evidence demonstrating that natural communication methodologies are more effective in teaching the written and oral aspects of an FL than are other methodologies [e.g., the audio-lingual method]. Rather, studies seem to indicate that for poor FL learners, direct teaching of the phonological, orthographic [and grammatical rule] system is essential. (p. 253)*

It would not be out of line, then, to claim that students with learning difficulties in Immersion might be ill-suited to a highly communicative methodology. Perhaps, the ordered and gradual presentation of the different basic syntactic and grammatical rules and vocabulary might ease their burden and enable them to progress in a more efficient and less painful way. Incomprehensible input from texts and inaccurate output from students can certainly contribute to give the at-risk students a damaging feeling of frustration and helplessness. For them, immersing can be equal to drowning. So, unlike the more recent research on language learning that places emphasis on comprehension and production of language, these children might need a more structured approach to language learning. Campbell (1992) interviewed a teacher with 15 years of experience in Immersion. He reports that this teacher believed that "there are many problems in French Immersion which cause children to feel like failures because they haven't learned certain aspects of the language. These problems stem from…a lack of systematic grammatical instruction" (p. 195).

So, evidently, some learners prefer to treat language analytically and they might be more successful if they were allowed "to play to their strengths" (Skehan, 1991, p. 279). This different syllabus might then help in creating a sense of security and well-being and in encouraging the children along the language acquisition path.

As seen earlier, it has been claimed that children with learning difficulties in Immersion would encounter similar hardship, were they educated in the majority language; however, parents' reports also bear testimony to their children's experience of a lighter burden and happier disposition once switched to a unilingual environment (Bonyun, Morrison, Unitt, 1981; Parkin, Morrison, Watkin, 1987; Waterston, 1990). Some parents would also prefer to see their children develop a firm foundation in English language skills before letting them start in Immersion. According to Diaz (1982), children have different second language abilities and it is possible that during the initial period of second language learning, "one could observe the most dramatic, and perhaps negative effects on young second language learners" (p. 11). He adds:

> *The available evidence suggests the hypothesis that bilingualism might have both positive and negative effects on cognitive development depending on the level of competence a bilingual child attains in his or her two languages. If the hypothesis is true, one could expect some rather harsh cognitive consequences for those children who fail to overcome the initial difficulties of coping with two languages. (p. 12)*

Incidentally, it is interesting to see how Lapkin, one of the authors of *Immersion: The Trial Balloon That Flew*, extolled then the advantages of early bilingual education, but began in 1989 to express doubt as to whether Early Immersion is the best choice for most children: "I used to say so with more confidence than I do now" (Nicolson, 1989, p. 34, in *Today's Parent*).

Vygotskyan Theory of Learning

As seen earlier, Cummins (1984) recommends a "reciprocal interaction" model of pedagogy (p. 224) that emphasizes "genuine dialogue between student and teacher, and guidance and facilitation rather than control of student learning by the teacher" (p. 224). This natural and meaningful interaction, says Cummins (1984), is:

> *congruent both with theories of cognitive development that stress action on the environment as the crucial process in the development of cognitive operations [e.g., Piaget] and with those that emphasize social interaction as the matrix within which higher level thought processes*

develop [e.g., Vygotsky]. (p. 230)

Unfortunately, Immersion students are not immersed among native speakers of the target language. Often, these students live in an English-speaking environment that does not provide opportunity for communicating in French, and the classroom set-up represents a very artificial learning arrangement. Consequently, one cannot claim that the learning of the second language mimics that of the mother tongue; it cannot be claimed either that genuine "social interaction" (p. 230) is taking place often enough during the school day between every child and the sole target language speaker of the classroom. Even though most students learn the second language reasonably well under such circumstances, others experience difficulties which can also be explained by Vygotsky's theory of learning.

In order to handle these difficulties, the teacher must know (according to the Vygotskyan theory of learning) what level the learners are at, or what their Zone of Proximal Development (ZPD) is. The ZPD represents "the difference between what the child, or novice, is capable of when acting alone and what he or she is capable of when acting under the guidance of a more experienced other" (Lantolf & Appel, 1994, p. 10). By responding to the assistance of the more experienced member of society, the learner enters into a "dialogic interaction" (Aljaafreh & Lantolf, 1994, p. 467). This activity is "essentially a mediated process" (Aljaafreh & Lantolf, 1994, p. 467) to encourage the learner to function at his potential level of ability. As a result, the learner is expected to internalize or appropriate the new knowledge and accomplish tasks he was unable to accomplish alone before. Thus, the teacher helps the learner proceed from the inter-mental domain[4] of the assisted performance to the intra-mental domain[5] of the internalization of the new knowledge. It is at this internalization point that the learner reaches actual development (as opposed to potential development). However, the potential development is more important than the actual development because it indicates the readiness of the learner to experience more mental growth and to further advance his actual development. Students who experience learning difficulties cannot learn on their own; they must receive performance assistance from the teacher and help is most effective when it is provided on an individual basis "according to the exigencies of the moment and movement through the ZPD" (Gallimore & Tharp, 1990, p. 183).

In terms of teacher assistance, the learners would benefit from information on their performance. When learning a second language, learners also need feedback about accuracy, for unless feedback is provided, no correction or even maintenance is possible. "Standards for performance can be exemplified by the teacher instructing the children to repeat the process until accuracy is achieved" (Gallimore & Tharp, 1990, p. 180). According to Aljaafreh and Lantolf (1994), studies have demonstrated that error correction or negative feedback can influence positively the learning process: "L2 learners provided with corrective feedback do indeed outperform control groups given minimal or no negative input" (p. 566). Carroll and Swain (1993) think that explicit feedback could be more beneficial than implicit negative correction because the former identifies the precise location and nature of errors whereas the latter requires the learner to engage in a great deal of guesswork. Likewise, corrective feedback, if it is to have any impact on the learning process, has to be attuned to the individual learner. "This process is thus one of continuous *assessment* of the novice's needs and abilities and the *tailoring* of help to those conditions" (Aljaafreh & Lantolf, 1994, p. 468). Oxford and Shearin (1996) say:

> *Vygotsky's work implies that L2 learning goals must be clearly based on learners' needs and interests for motivation to occur, and the input from the teacher must be both relevant and demanding. If these stipulations are not met, progress through the zone of proximal development will be stunted. (p. 138)*

In other words, the students with learning difficulties need to receive the appropriate help that would allow them to function without finding the learning task frustrating. When the level of ability of these students does not match that required by the Immersion classroom where, as we have seen, the emphasis is placed on communication and on comprehension and production of language, with the understanding that the right forms of language will be acquired implicitly, these students simply do not acquire the right forms of the language. In fact, their actual linguistic development is not being taken into account and their zone of proximal development, which indicates the level they are capable of functioning at, is totally ignored. What is more, when confronted with the increasingly complex decontextualized linguistic nature of the instructional material (meant for Francophones), and required to read and learn from texts that offer what seems like incomprehensible information, these students experience great difficulties and distress. Consequently, they are not acquiring meaning; in fact, their poverty of language not only interferes with further linguistic progress, but it seriously impedes the understanding of other school subjects taught through the medium of the second language. At this point, these students are not receiving the appropriate level of assistance and are not encouraged to function at their actual level of competence. They are not being helped in their ZPD.

Oxford and Shearin (1996), in reviewing Vygotsky's contributions in the realm of socio-cultural cognition, mention: "When the learner needs the greatest assistance, the teacher provides 'scaffolding' to ensure that the learner's constructs will continue to grow stronger and more complex" (p. 137). However, students experiencing language learning difficulties possess an actual developmental level of that language that does not correspond to the general level of the classroom. Therefore, they cannot benefit from the performance assistance that is provided in the classroom. These children's "scaffolding"[6] of linguistic growth and development is not being provided; they need individual help; they need assistance at their personal level of potential development.

It is easy to understand how, then, undermined by sinking feelings of anxiety and hopelessness, they reach for safer grounds within an all-English environment, where help is more readily available, either through the school administration, or their own Anglophone parents.

I would suggest that students with learning difficulties would probably benefit from cognitive structuring that provides a structure for understanding and sequencing perception, memory and action. Sequencing of both old and new information could be very helpful as well. The goal would be to help students understand how the different parts of the language relate to one another. It is also important that children's experience of the second language be evaluated correctly and the learning activities be chosen judiciously so as to accommodate the level of the learners' proximal development. Williams and Burden (1997) advise: "Tasks should be made optimally challenging by taking into account each individual's zone of next potential" (p. 139). Students enjoy activities which are within their ability and are presented at a pace appropriate to their learning style; they need teaching that takes their level into account (Greenspan, 1997).

Furthermore, students should be able to find the appropriate individual mediated assistance and the corrective feedback that would allow them to progress through their zone of proximal development. Some children do experience learning difficulties when they find themselves in a linguistic medium they cannot handle and Wiss (1989) suggests that "the crucial factors are the environment and the method of instruction....The challenge to educators is to provide reliable and valid methods and materials so that all children who desire bi-literacy skills have access to them" (p. 528). She further urges researchers "to seek models for the early recognition of potential learning problems in French Immersion and the best way to handle these problems on an *individual basis*" (p. 528) (my emphasis).

Individuals are different in their cognitive potentials and their learning styles. Education would permit more learners to succeed if it were:

> *tailored to the abilities and the needs of the particular individuals involved. Indeed, the cost of attempting to treat all individuals the same, or of trying to convey knowledge to individuals in ways uncongenial to their preferred modes of learning, may be great. (Gardner, 1985, p. 385)*

Chapter VI.
Second Language Learning:
Individual Differences and Difficulties

In order to better understand the learning difficulties of some students in the Immersion program, and perhaps entice educators into finding better ways of tailoring the learning environment to the abilities and needs of particular individuals, this chapter proposes to look at what influences the second language learning process and where the difficulties might originate from. If the Immersion program is not suitable for everyone, perhaps this can be attributed to the learners' different individual responses to the second language learning experience. Differences (Skehan, 1991) due to different abilities, physiological, cognitive or affective, could affect the kind of participation the learner brings to the learning situation.

Factors Influencing Second Language Learning

Anyone teaching languages or observing children in the process of learning a language in a natural environment quickly becomes aware of progress variation in second language acquisition. In the classroom, students can soon be identified as belonging to three major groups: the successful ones who seem to absorb with great ease the vocabulary, the structures and the pronunciation of the new language, the average ones who tug along with a great deal of conscious effort and the unsuccessful ones who stumble over every aspect of language acquisition. Individual second language learning differences have been attributed to numerous influential factors. These are cognitive and affective influences such as intelligence and motivation and character traits such as extroversion/introversion, anxiety and risk-taking dispositions. They also include match or mismatch of learning environment and students' learning styles, which can be influenced by brain hemisphericity, field dependence/independence[1] or distinct preferences for auditory, visual or kinesthetic types of learning material. It is beyond the scope of this thesis to examine every character trait or the many learning strategies that set apart *good* from *bad* learners. Let us only briefly mention that

Skehan (1989, 1991) reported studies of successful language learners' cognitive and meta-cognitive strategies which failed to provide any help to the unsuccessful students who attempted to adopt them:

> *Currently, despite the enormous energies and talent that have gone into developing strategy training materials, there has been relatively little evidence of a gain-score nature to indicate the effectiveness of such training.... There is still the worrying possibility that good learners are ones for whom the use of effective strategies are possible, while for poorer learners they are not. (Skehan, 1991, p. 287-288)*

This revelation may bring more evidence to a relationship between individual differences and a certain predisposition toward second language learning. Campbell (1992) relates the example of a child with learning difficulties in Immersion whose mother believed that learning languages is easier for some people than others. She herself had experienced great difficulty in learning French while growing up in Quebec; she still could not speak the language, yet, her sisters learned it very easily.

We may then be tempted to conclude that there exists a particular innate foreign language aptitude – a knack for languages. Gajar (1987) mentions that there is a strong belief among language teachers and psychologists that a unique linguistic aptitude distinct from general intelligence underlies the successful learning of a foreign language.

Influence of IQ or IQ Influenced?

Does IQ influence language learning or does language learning eventually affect IQ? The debate over cause-effect relations between degree of bilingualism and cognitive ability and growth has been going on for a long time. As we have seen earlier, in the past, bilingualism was thought to exert negative effects on cognitive development (Macnamara, 1966). On the other hand, the bilingual child appeared intellectually superior (Peal and Lambert, 1962). But then, these authors could not definitely say whether this intellectually superior child became bilingual because of intelligence or whether bilingualism helped intellectual development. Barik and Swain's (1976) French Immersion findings "do not support the general trend of studies by other investigators who have found positive effects of bilingualism on cognitive growth" (p. 259), except for the high French achievers, those who attain a relatively high degree of proficiency in the second language and who are thus able to reap greater cognitive growth. The ambiguity lives on as Diaz' (1982) studies support the claim that bilingualism fosters the development of cognitive abilities, whereas Bernhard (1993) thinks it would be impossible to determine whether the advantages found in association with bilingualism are directly related to the effects of knowing a second language or due to pre-existing cognitive differences between bilingual and unilingual subjects.

In an IQ comparison study of French Immersion and non-Immersion students, Olson and Burns (1983) found that "no one in the French Immersion group scored below 115 in a population in which 71 percent of the regular English stream were below this level" (p. 4). According to a report given at a French Immersion Symposium held in Ottawa in 1995, out of 100 children who enter Immersion in Kindergarten (in the Carleton-Ottawa area), only 15 to 20 graduate with a bilingual diploma. Among the latter, one finds that 50% of them achieve an average mark of over 80% and that 24 to 30% of them are identified as intellectually gifted. Also, 95% of these students are university bound. As well, in an article of *Today's Parent* (April, 1999), Krueger[2] mentions:

> *A recent study of graduating Immersion students in Alberta, for example, showed they had higher average scores in all subjects than their peers in English-language programs. Of course, this could reflect the fact that learning-disabled students are filtered out of Immersion and high achievers are put into it. (p. 34)*

What this means, is that children who enter Immersion and stay long enough to graduate are likely to display more academic ability.

Nevertheless, whether intelligence helps in developing bilingualism or bilingualism helps in developing cognitive abilities, it is now well known that intelligence does not represent the only or most important factor of second language learning; it does not guarantee its success either (Genesee, 1992). Mandel and Marcus (1995) mention that intelligence is only one of many factors that influence successful school results: "don't assume for one second that just because your child is intelligent, high marks will automatically follow....Research clearly shows that no individual's capabilities and talents are equally distributed across the board" (p. 10). Both Burstall (1976) and Rivers (1976) relate examples of students identified as possessing above average academic ability and yet, unsuccessful at learning a foreign language. Some of the academically gifted students of Burstall (1976) and Rivers (1976) experienced a hard time coping with the "intolerable" (p. 212) oral form of the foreign language. On the other hand, some of Rivers' (1976) low general scholastic ability students seemed to possess an extraordinary "intuitive" (p. 214) ability in listening comprehension. In other studies, Ganschow, Sparks and Javorsky (1998) find that students with and without foreign language learning difficulties do not differ significantly in their level of IQ.

As far as students in the Immersion program are concerned, there is research evidence (Cummins, 1986) that their IQ does not relate any more significantly to success than it does for students in the regular English stream. The Immersion type of education does not suit only children of above average intelligence, for below average students are quite capable of achieving similar results in terms of pronunciation, fluency and interpersonal communication skills. But, it is my experience that both students of above and below average ability greatly differ in their degree of bilingual achievement; this difference becomes especially salient at the level of literacy acquisition. Hamayan, Genesee and Tucker (1977) also speak of individual variations within French language learning groups:

> *Thus, although the pupils participating in the bilingual programs described above (French Immersion) have developed as a group, far greater facility in French than English pupils who have followed a conventional French-as-a-second language program, it is nevertheless the case that there exists a wide range of variation in the French proficiency of both Immersion students and pupils in conventional programs. (p. 227)*

Carroll (1981) distinguishes between aptitude or a state of capability and achievement or outcome of the learning task. Carroll (1981) also notes that although foreign language aptitude, the ability to acquire languages easily and quickly, relates to some aspects of intelligence, it does not always correlate with the expected corresponding level of achievement; it is not as much a determinant of success as other more influential factors. In this respect, Norton and Toohey (in press) approach the explanation of successful language learning on the basis of "access to a variety of conversations" in the community rather than on the basis of control or speed of acquisition of "a wider variety of linguistic forms and meanings" (p. 5). They see language learning "not so much as a gradual and neutral process of internalizing the rules, structures, and vocabulary of a standard language," but rather as learners' appropriation of "the utterances of others in historical and cultural practices, situated in particular communities" (p. 6). According to Norton and Toohey (in press), good language learners exercise their agency in using "a variety of resources to gain access to their peer networks" and "pay attention to social practices" (p. 11-13) of the target language environment. Society's response to learners' actions either facilitates or blocks the development of the second language.

And so, it has been claimed that success in learning a foreign language depends more on the learner's motivation, personality and attitude than on her intelligence.

Influence of Motivation or Motivation Influenced?

Without totally yielding to the above view or downplaying the importance of the underlying cognitive advantage of aptitude, it is true that highly motivated individuals want to learn the language and consequently apply themselves diligently at the foreign language learning task, whether they find it hard or not. According to Gardner and Lambert (1972), these individuals most probably feel empathy and interest toward the ethnic group of the target language; they show a willingness to adopt another language and culture and to participate in the ethnic community's activities. Such open-mindedness and integrative attitudinal/motivational factors play a major role in achieving proficiency in the other language. They are also more effective than other factors of instrumental motivation geared toward professional advancement and based on benefits and advantages that can be accrued from knowing another language. Gardner and Lambert (1972) attribute the effective factors of integrative motivation to the personality of the learner. Genesee (1987) concurs with them in recognizing the weightier influence of attitudinal/motivational factors: "It follows then that students other than the intellectually gifted can master a second language in school by virtue of positive attitudes and motivation" (p. 82). And so, while some students of above average intelligence sometimes fail to acquire a foreign language, others of lower ability succeed, thanks to the positive affective variables of attitude and motivation.[3]

But motivation does not always work in a simple manner and when evaluating the role of motivation, one must remember to include the influence of external sources of motivation. This influence is ambivalent and multivariate in character, and highly susceptible to change depending on factors such as rewards, constraints, emotional state of the learner, type of instruction and instructor as well as learning situation and conditions.

However, expanding the motivation construct, Tremblay and Gardner (1995) find that all the motivational factors including the desire to learn the language or the satisfactions one derives from learning the language (either in the target language environment or in the classroom), do not really reflect true motivation unless they are accompanied by a great deal of effort, attention and persistence. Nevertheless, in language teaching, we often come across individuals who seem able to acquire a foreign language fairly easily even when not particularly motivated to do so and other individuals who, despite their high motivation, interest and persistent effort, experience great difficulty in attaining a successful level of bilingual competence. Therefore, one could also concede at this point that learners who experience success might feel encouraged to try harder, whereas those who experience a lack of success might feel discouraged and stop persisting. As Skehan (1989, 1991) notes: motivation could be a consequence rather than a cause of success.

So, like IQ, motivation, whether it be intrinsic or extrinsic, does not guarantee success either. It appears then, that the existence of a unique linguistic aptitude may not be so fictitious after all and that the discouraging lack of success, when not attributable to a lack of motivation or IQ, could very well have its origin in specific foreign language disabilities. But before we deal with the latter, let us examine another influential factor of individual second language learning differences.

Crippling or Facilitating Anxiety?

In reference to the above-mentioned emotional state of the learner, one affective variable that also exerts an important influential force on the language learning process is anxiety. Horwitz, Horwitz and Cope (1991) first describe anxiety in general as "the subjective feeling of tension, apprehension, nervousness, and worry associated with an arousal of the autonomic nervous system" (p. 27).[4] This condition, when experienced in the language class, can prevent many otherwise good learners from becoming successful language learners. In fact, Horwitz et al. (1991) conceive of a very specific foreign language anxiety, "a distinct complex of self-perceptions, beliefs, feelings and behaviors related to classroom language learning arising from the uniqueness of the language learning process" (p. 31).

The relationship between anxiety and classroom performance presents a fairly complex picture and raises a question of causality: does anxiety interfere with language learning ability and lead to poor performance or does it emerge as a consequence of poor performance? First of all, it is not easy to differentiate between a permanent state of anxiety that understandably and invariably affects the language learning process in a negative way and a specific type of anxiety that the learning of a language is capable of provoking in some individuals. In the latter case, the anxiety experience can act either as a crippler or as a facilitator. This is how some students, feeling anxious from the time they start a language course, manage to experience success despite or probably because of the initial anxiety. On the other hand, other students, whose learning outcome does not match their anticipations, can become quite anxious later in the course; in turn, their anxiety will further impinge on their progress. Ehrman (1996) finds a close link between motivation, self-efficacy and anxiety:

> *Satisfactory self-efficacy contributes to maintenance and even enhancement of motivation.... On the other hand, disappointment with one's performance can lead to reduced self-efficacy and also to reduced motivation; it can also result in anxiety that gets in the way of learning. (p. 148)*

According to Scovel (1978), the combination of the difficulty of the learning task and the IQ of the students also plays a correlating role in the emergence of either a positive or negative type of anxiety. High IQ students tend to benefit from a certain level of anxiety that seems to promote success and form the underpinning of a strong motivation and positive attitudes. Conversely, lower IQ students feel hampered by an anxiety which provides more negative re-inforcement and discouragement than anything else.

It is my personal experience that debilitating anxiety is present among students with learning difficulties in the French Immersion program, whether these students be of lower or higher IQ. This anxiety often transpires through skipping, avoiding homework and not being able to study or to concentrate in class:

> *Facilitating anxiety motivates the learner to 'fight' the new learning task; it gears the learner emotionally for approach behavior. Debilitating anxiety, in contrast motivates the learner to 'flee' the new learning task; it stimulates the individual emotionally to adopt avoidance behavior (Scovel, 1978, p. 139).*

The debilitating anxiety most probably finds its source in the students' own recognition of language learning problems. The realization of the existence of a learning obstacle can be very disconcerting and frustrating to well-motivated students, especially those planning to further their education in institutions of higher learning with a second language credit entrance prerequisite. In their studies, Ganschow and Sparks (1995) have obtained results suggesting that poor second language learners exhibit higher levels of anxiety as a consequence rather than as a cause of their basic problems with language. According to these authors, affective comportment of high anxiety, low motivation and negative attitudes are the inevitable outcome of the oral and written language difficulties. Anxiety in particular appears as a likely byproduct of the interrelation between the learner's skills and the cognitive demands of the language learning task. "In the affective domain, our research suggests that poor attitude and lack of motivation are a result of difficulties with language, rather than a cause of Foreign Language learning problems" (p. 248). Dinklage (1991) also proposes that the emotional block, often suspected of causing learning problems, is rather a rare occurrence. "Language disabilities cause emotional problems, are complicated and made worse by emotional problems, but seldom have I seen a specific language disability caused primarily by emotional problems" (p. 3).

So, what actually prevents some students from learning a language as efficiently as others? Ehrman (1996) wonders if it is the lack of an innate foreign language aptitude or rather the existence of various learning disabilities in the shape of biological or physiological obstacles? On one hand, according to Dinklage (1991), when a student experiences difficulties in language learning, usually, all that is needed is a reasonable amount of compensatory effort. But on the other hand, "where this effort has reached unreasonable bounds and where the yield from the effort is so atypically inadequate, it is probable that something special is at work" (p. 6).

Likely Sources of Learning Disabilities

What could that "something special at work" be?

It has been suggested in the literature that a foreign language learning disability does not exist in isolation and that foreign language learning problems correlate with other learning disabilities. The term learning disability often refers to a range of biologically based difficulties that create a significant discrepancy between estimated learning potential and actual performance (Ehrman, 1996). Ehrman divides the common learning disabilities into four categories: input – integration – memory – and output. The visual and auditory perceptual disabilities that belong to the input category include difficulties with depth perception, orientation in space, eye-body coordination and sound differentiation and processing. Sequencing (of ideas or events), simultaneous processing (multitasking) and abstraction (seeing interrelation or going from specific to general) belong to the integration category. Difficulties in this category will be felt differentially according to the individuals' visual or auditory perception of data. Short-term and long-term memory difficulties for which numerous repetitions are needed (short-term) or retrieval of data which is slow and difficult (long-term) belong to the memory category. In the output category, we find difficulties with words (production or reception and reading), motor activities (movements of groups of muscles), numbers (computing and calculating). This latter disability is often referred to as dyscalculia, whereas the term dyslexia refers more commonly to a reading disability.

There have always been students with learning disabilities who experience tremendous difficulties in certain courses. For instance, some students find great difficulty in spelling correctly, others can't seem to memorize their multiplication tables, even though they excel in their computer science courses; others still have trouble with the reading of maps or graphs. Besides their learning disability, these students often possess a high intelligence and special talents in areas other than that of their disability. Presumably, this disability is due to "a neurological miswiring in the brain" (Pompian, 1986, p.1) which makes it difficult for students to process information for specific tasks. In terms of second language learning difficulties, this "miswiring" would affect the auditory short term memory of the students and render meaningless the different sounds of words and phrases they hear.

The signs of underlying learning disabilities have only been briefly stated here. In fact, disabilities, because of their many forms and combinations and degrees of severity, are difficult to diagnose. As well, their impact on the individual's life escapes assessment. However difficult these learning disabilities may be to recognize, their impact in the second language classroom should not be taken lightly. Ehrman (1996) thinks that "Learning disabilities and classroom foreign language learning are a notoriously unpromising combination" (p. 267). She produces citations from Barr (1993) and Levine (1987), who respectively state that "Recent findings show that most students with learning disabilities have inordinate difficulties in foreign language classes"[5] and that "No single content area is as commonly a threat to (*students*) with learning difficulties as is that of foreign languages."[6] Evidently, the learning disabilities (referred to as LD from now on) associated with foreign language learning are more specifically related to native language based deficits found in any of the above four categories. In other words, first language limitations, whether they be physiological or biological, will also hinder foreign language acquisition.

Specific Foreign Language Difficulties

The inability to master a foreign language can be very frustrating and demoralizing, especially when the learning struggle takes so much time and effort away from other subject areas. Levine (1987) observes that "for certain students, learning a foreign language is an anathema. They may work exceedingly hard only to discover that their minds reject a second language as vigorously as their bodies might reject a skin graft" (p. 375).

Most research by foreign language educators on difficulties in the acquisition of a second language has focused on such variables as intelligence, aptitude, attitude, motivation and anxiety. Gajar (1987) mentions that studies addressing the existence or diagnosis of a specific foreign language disability are scarce; however, a review of the literature confirms its existence. Foreign language training schools conducted by the military have reported attrition rates as high as 80%. As well, there are students who repeatedly fail their foreign language courses despite their high degree of motivation and academic aptitude. Lefebvre (1984) reports that during a 3 year program at the University of Virginia, approximately 75% of the 97 students referred to the Learning Needs and Evaluation Center (LNEC) were initially referred because of foreign language difficulties. Given an intellectual cognitive assessment with the WAIS-R[7] Information and Vocabulary sub-tests, 46 of them scored significantly lower than LD referrals for other academic problems. Lefebvre says: "These results suggest impaired language skills that may affect learning a new language" (p. 362).

Anyway, Ganschow, Sparks et al. (1991) indicate that 78% of colleges and universities have policies that allow students who experience extreme difficulties in learning foreign languages to waive or substitute the foreign language requirement under certain circumstances. Dinklage (1991) writes:

> *It turns out that for all of its elitism and academic conservatism Harvard was the first college, as far as I have been able to determine, to recognize that they might have in their midst learning disabled students for whom special accommodation was needed and which was then in fact provided. What we are talking about is that in 1959 Harvard began taking a close look at those students who could not pass a foreign language class no matter how smart they were or how hard they studied. (p. 1)*

Referring to students who seem unable to learn a second language and "spend numerous hours struggling in vain" (p. 382), Levine (1987) suggests that "Ultimately, the wasted time and anxiety begin to erode other subject areas as well" (p. 382). He proposes:

> *At some point, it seems appropriate to call a halt to such a losing effort. It is certainly not worth sacrificing a child's academic career for the sake of a foreign language. High schools and colleges must become alert to this phenomenon. (p. 382)*

As seen earlier, attempts have been made to attribute the failure to learn a second language to the cognitive functioning level of the students or their affective dispositions, such as high anxiety, low motivation and negative attitudes. However, Ganschow and Sparks (1998) speculate that all these affective comportments are more symptomatic of language learning problems. In the last few years, attention has been given to physiological variables, particularly those which might be responsible for problems in the receptive domain (sound discrimination, verbal memory, grammatical sensitivity). Spolsky (1989) states that "any physiological or biological limitations that block the learning of a first language will similarly block the learning of a second language" (p. 89).

Physiological and Biological Limitations

Dinklage (1971) relates cases of Harvard students who never got anything but an A in any school course except their language course, for which no amount of hard work yielded the success they experienced in other subjects, even after several repeats of the course. Some of these students had difficulty discriminating between similar but different sounds; in fact, this discrimination sometimes "exists to such a degree as to constitute a disability specific to the matter of learning a foreign language" (p. 195). According to Lavine and Schwartz (1996), many highly educated people cannot learn foreign languages and even being conversationally bilingual does not preclude language learning disabilities either.

Pimsleur, Sundland and McIntyre (1964) indicate that there exists evidence of a special *auditory ability* related to language learning achievement (p. 135). They conclude that "Low auditory ability is apparently an important factor both in foreign under-achievement and in the dropout problem" (p. 136). On the subject of abilities, Greenspan (1997) claims that variations in a baby's nervous system, musculature or sense organs may keep a child from developing a given ability. We do know, adds Greenspan (1997), that "the functioning of the senses varies from individual to individual, and so does sensory experience" (p. 48). This is why every child comprehends and reacts to the different types of sensation in a particular and personal way. "When we observe both older children and adults, it is difficult not to notice the range of differences in how people experience sensory aliveness" (Greenspan, 1997, p. 50).

The attempts to explain second language learning difficulties reflect diverse points of view. Carroll (1981), in his search for the foreign language learning "knack," finally presumed that "aptitudes reside deep within the individual's biological constitution and manifest themselves only indirectly in the process of learning and performance" (p. 87). Levine (1987) attributes second language learning difficulties to deficiencies of active memory and retrieval (p. 379). Service (1992) also recognizes the important role of working memory in learning new language material, so this new material can later be found in the long-term memory.

Day and Shapson (1983) mention that among the reasons given for transferring out of Immersion, school principals cite specific learning difficulties such as poor auditory memory. Lasky and Katz (1983) have proposed to examine the problem of second language learning difficulty from a central auditory processing perspective (CAP) or what they consider to be "the manipulation and utilization of sound signals by the central nervous system – what we do with what we hear" (p. 4). They suggest that academic problems of children could stem from difficulties in listening and understanding auditory information; in other words, difficulties in processing and analyzing auditory linguistic information (p. 5). This would affect the way they attend, follow and remember directions. Lasky (1983) finds that the personal characteristics that learners bring to the task of listening also influence the auditory processing system. Variables such as "linguistic and socio-linguistic competence, expectations, interests, and motivation" (p. 24) are relevant to CAP and affect the child's listening strategies. As well, a central auditory processing disorder can lead to failure and criticism and eventually to an emotional trauma (Hoffman, 1983). CAP disorders, according to Byrne and Lester (1983) also exist among children with above average and superior intelligence.

Horwitz (1991) mentions that some language learners claim to hear only "a loud buzz" (p. 29) when their teacher speaks the foreign language; they have difficulty discriminating the sound and the structures of the target language. Some of my Immersion students who have been in the program for ten years also complain of not being able to understand the messages of the films presented to them in class; a second and third viewing of some important scenes to give them another chance to "hear" does not seem to help much either. Dinklage (1991) claims that there are students "without very serious reading or spelling problems," who do have "unusually poor auditory discrimination and/or auditory memory" because they cannot "differentiate between similar but different sounds" (p. 2). He adds: "Those with auditory processing deficits are also particularly bamboozled by foreign accents, especially where the language is the teacher's native tongue" (p. 4). M. Stern (1991) states as well that the tests and psychological reports administered to children who demonstrate lack of progress in Immersion provide evidence that these children suffer from auditory and linguistic processing difficulties:

> *The following areas of weakness were noted: auditory discrimination (the ability to discriminate between similar sounding words), auditory memory (the ability to remember information that is heard), auditory expressive skills (the ability to reproduce orally or on paper material that has been heard), phonics (putting sounds together), auditory visual association (the ability to associate auditory and visual material that is necessary to gain meaning from the environment), receptive language (the ability to understand what is said to you), expressive language (the ability to express orally what you want to say), and reversals (spatial and sequencing difficulties). (p. 127)*

Dube (1993) also notes that some parents blame auditory perception problems, poor memory and confusion with sounds for their children's difficulties in the Immersion program.

Nonetheless, a general lack of linguistic and meta-linguistic awareness or a diminished sensitivity to the speech-sound structure of language leads to problems in the native language as well – problems such as reading and listening comprehension difficulties and written language deficits (in grammar, spelling and writing). According to Ganschow, Sparks et al. (1991), not only does the ability to use a phonological[8] code give access to reading acquisition and achievement in the native language, but this ability extends to foreign language learning also. This link between native and foreign language relates to good and poor foreign language learners, to their efficient or non-efficient use of phonology, syntax and semantics. However, it is specific linguistic coding problems at the phonological and syntactic levels, these authors propose, that create the greatest difficulty for foreign language students. My Immersion students, Michael, Kevin and David, had difficulty in their English language course and also hated to read or write. Ganschow, Sparks et al. (1991) claim that these phonological and syntactic coding deficits (later termed differences)[9] can also affect the non LD student.[10]

Chapter VII:
Second Language Learning and First Language Proficiency

A conversation I had with an Immersion kindergarten teacher led me to believe that learning difficulties evident at that grade level were often a predictor of future failure for some children. Perhaps we have assumed, with too much confidence, that all who learnt their native tongue so easily could also learn a foreign language just as easily.

This chapter proposes to look at the interrelationship of native and foreign language skills. All children do not acquire their first language processing skills (phonological, orthographic, syntactic and semantic) at the same rate and this earlier developmental difference may very well account not only for later differences in native language skills, but also for the difference in foreign language aptitude (Ganschow, Sparks et al., 1991).

Importance and Role of First Language

The Immersion program was not designed for minority language children or for children who join school with no or limited proficiency in English. However, because of their different socio-economic backgrounds or language problems (e.g., speech delay or impediment), majority language (English) children come to school endowed with diverse first language abilities. These abilities underlie the degree of success they are likely to achieve in school, for the development of language skills is highly correlated with other cognitive skills (Carroll, 1993). Well's 1985 Bristol Project, mentioned by Skehan (1989), reports "massive individual differences" (p. 31 and p. 37) in the rate of children's language development – differences that schooling unfortunately seems to "consolidate" (p. 31) rather than remove. Much learning in school is mediated through language and children with delayed or in-complete first language development often do poorly in school. Therefore, one could expect that these same children would experience even more difficulty when schooled in a different language; a less developed first language proficiency could indeed represent a disadvantage in early bilingual education.

How do we know to what extent the child's language is functioning in the full sense? Children may very well understand much of what is said to them and they may easily produce meaningful language, but it would be a mistake to assume that this linguistic ability demonstrates their overall language skills. "Some children with relatively mild or sub-clinical language disabilities may ultimately have learned to comprehend and express themselves in their native language because they have been so overexposed to it" (Melvin, 1987, p. 378). While all children acquire oral language, they do not develop all language skills at the same rate. The children's experience of their first language as a communicative tool in interpersonal contexts does not necessarily mean they are yet able to use confidently their language as a cognitive tool that would allow them to cope in the Immersion program (Weininger, 1982). In other words, a solid foundation in the first language is an absolute prerequisite for a successful acquisition of a second language. The same conceptual thinking is reflected in Hayden's (1988) recommendation of a later Immersion program for the at-risk children whose mother tongue literacy development is less advanced than that of their peers in the early grades.

However, Bruck (1982) is of the opinion that the poor language development of some children should not stop them from getting access to the Immersion program, since like all children, they can tap the natural language learning abilities they all possess. Both Bruck (1982) and Genesee (1992) have concluded that children who are at risk because of their lesser first language ability do not experience additional difficulties in the Immersion program. They also agree that the children enjoy an added benefit in terms of improved second language proficiency. On the other hand, on the basis of conflicting evidence, Weininger (1982) thinks that:

> Relationships between mother-tongue and second-language development at the earliest stages are more complex than is suggested by the broad assumption that the child is sufficiently 'flexible' to develop linguistically on the two separate tracks provided by the home-school language switch. (p. 29)

He also expresses concern regarding children who experience a difficult time while trying to cope with the two languages: "In the present state of knowledge, I think we should not be too confident in assuming that the advantage of learning the second language compensates for other disadvantages such children experience" (p. 33).

The disadvantaged students may indeed develop, in the beginning, similar speaking and listening skills as their more advantaged peers; nevertheless, as mentioned earlier, they soon encounter difficulties that curtail further progress. Consequently, the testimony of reports from dropouts, their parents and teachers (previously mentioned), leads me to believe that researchers such as Bruck and Genesee may have been too hasty in their conclusions.

Cummins' Hypotheses

Cummins (1978) explains the poor achievement results of children with learning difficulties in Immersion on the basis of their first language developmental stage. Cummins believes that children who have achieved a high level of competence in their first language (L1) will also develop a similar level of competence in their second language (L2). Majority language (English) children in Immersion programs undergo an "additive" type of bilingualism, which as seen earlier helps them in attaining a high level of L2 competence without positing any threat to their L1. However, even though these majority language children are surrounded by a stimulating L1 environment inside and outside the home, some of them, from a lower socio-economic background, may have experienced language in a very functionally different manner by the time they start their schooling. These children may be quite fluent in the interpersonal functions of their L1, but not so cognitively competent in its logical functions – functions which are required for success in school. According to Cummins (1978), a minimal threshold level of competence in the first language must be attained at the beginning of the exposure to the L2 in order to develop competence in the L2 and avoid any negative cognitive effects. This developmental interdependence hypothesis suggests that competence in a second language is dependent upon the development stage of the mother tongue. In addition to this, when the first language is poorly developed, intensive exposure to a second language can impede further development of the first language skills. This, in turn, will exert a limiting effect on the development of the second language.

Thus, a second higher threshold of bilingual competence must be attained in order to reap the cognitive benefits of bilingualism. "According to these hypotheses, the effects of bilingualism will vary as a function of the levels of competence attained in L1 and L2, which are, in turn, determined by the social and educational context in which the languages are learned" (Cummins, 1978, p. 863).

The level of L1 competence intervenes in the attainment of a balanced bilingualism and the greater cognitive growth associated with it; and so, on the basis of this interdependence, maintenance and fostering of a child's first language is of critical importance. Cummins and Swain (1986), under the "Principle of first things first" (p. 101), consider that the child's first language plays a crucial role in her educational development:

> *ensure that the child's home language is adequately developed before worrying about progress in the second language. It implies that the first language is so instrumental to the emotional and academic well-being of the child, that its development must be seen as high, if not the highest priority in the early years of schooling. (p. 101)*

Cummins and Swain (1986) were mainly referring to minority language children when they wrote these words; nevertheless, it is my own personal opinion that these words could be equally applicable to some majority language children who lack a certain level of conceptual linguistic knowledge at the start of their intensive exposure to L2 in the classroom. Belonging to a majority culture and being taught in an additive bilingual environment may not necessarily exert an adverse effect on the academic, cognitive and linguistic development of the at-risk child, but it does not automatically bestow upon such a child the cognitive and linguistic abilities he needs to deal with two languages.

Failure to overcome the difficulties of coping with two languages may thus stem from a low level of first language linguistic competence. Furthermore, failure to reach the minimal threshold level of bilingual competence can affect majority language disabled children and eventually produce negative cognitive effects, especially when instruction in the second language is maintained for a long period of time. Beitel (1986) warns about this threat:

> *For some, the linguistic deficits in both languages may be so severe as to fall below the lower threshold level of bilingual competence, resulting in a failure to adapt to French Immersion programming. These*

youngsters' continued participation in a French Immersion program would lead to more cognitive and academic setbacks than if they were schooled in a regular English program. (p. 88)

First Language as Predictor of Foreign Language Potential

Although the importance of one's native language in predicting foreign language learning potential has not been extensively investigated by researchers (Sparks, Ganschow and Patton, 1995), it is nevertheless strongly suspected now that there exists a relationship between native and foreign language learning, and that children with learning disabilities or other learning difficulties experience problems in their native language that contribute to their inability to learn a second language.

Skehan (1989) had already suggested that there existed a relationship between first and second language learning capacity and that children's speed of first language development correlated with their aptitude for second language skills. In other words, aptitude for learning a second language is probably a "residue"[1] of first language learning capacity. Ganschow and Sparks (1991) observe a "linkage" between the difficulties of young children learning language – "difficulties learning phonics and in acquiring reading and spelling skills" (p. 50) and the difficulties they later encounter in foreign language learning.

Learning to Read: A First or Second Language Experience?

Considering the evident correlation that exists between languages, it is not surprising that controversy should exist over in which language (the second language or the native language) a child should first start to read. Kamin (1980) thinks that if a child is experiencing difficulty in learning to read in French, he would likely experience the same kind of difficulty learning to read in English. The problem "detected in French may not be a problem with the French language *per se*" (p. 37). Kamin's opinion is corroborated by Child (1989), who maintains that the concerns of teachers and parents over a too challenging or too confusing French Immersion program for the child with reading difficulties appear to lack empirical support. Her comparison of low achieving transfer students and Immersion students with equivalent students in the English stream leads her to conclude that the French Immersion program does not cause or contribute to the reading difficulties. Consequently, there is no need to transfer these children into the English program with the expectation that learning to read in the first language will improve their reading performance.

On the other hand, a survey conducted by the Saint Albert Catholic Schools in Alberta and reported by Dube (1993) reaches a totally different conclusion: "On the basis of our experience with many parents and teachers in our French Immersion program, formal instruction in reading should occur in the child's first language, English" (p. 43). Similarly, a 1991 UNESCO World Education Report mentions that the task of learning to read in a second language that is not well known yet can lead to frustration and failure. Consequently, the children should first master reading and writing in their mother tongue so they can later experience a smooth development of the same mastery in the second language.

Some children are not ready to deal with text language at the time reading instruction starts in school. The acquisition of reading skills in the context of two weak languages may create confusion and adverse linguistic effects (Beitel, 1986). Parkin, Morrison and Watkin (1987) explain that some Early Immersion children undergo their first reading experiences in their second language when they do not yet possess the readiness in their first language. This is contrary to widely accepted theories of reading instruction that stress the importance of building on what the children already know and on the stage of their first language development. The children who begin to read in their second language (French) do not possess as wide a range of vocabulary as they do in English and so, there does not seem to be much co-ordination between what the children know in their second language and the second language reading activities they are expected to perform. Also, because of the higher demands on the working memory that reading in a second language requires, reading disabled children will experience great difficulty in understanding what they are reading.

Ganschow, Sparks, Javorsky, Pohlman and Bishop-Marbury (1991) refer to the LD literature and studies to expose the additional problem of large deficits in listening comprehension exhibited by children with reading disability (p. 8). According to Ganschow, Sparks et al. (1991), researchers attribute the reading/writing performance problems to a deficient phonological awareness – "the ability to conceive of spoken words as a sequence of phonemic segments and the capacity to identify these segments in spoken words and syllables" (p. 8). This phonological component affects first language acquisition and causes reading disability in children who possess a limited sensitivity to the speech-sound structure of the language. Furthermore, remark Ganschow, Sparks et al. (1991): "specific difficulty at the phoneme level can cause difficulties with the acquisition of oral and written language in both the native and the foreign language" (p. 9). Beitel (1986) also recognizes the importance of phonological awareness: "Establishment of word awareness and of phonological awareness may be further exacerbated by a confusion between the two languages and a severe delay in the acquisition of the French" (p. 88). In other words, the development of reading skills in a second language correlates strongly with the learners' competence in their first language. This interdependence of languages is of significant importance when trying to understand the learning difficulties of some Immersion students.

Stern (1991) relates the example of an Immersion student who experienced great difficulty due to a lack of good language and auditory skills; the psychologist who examined this child recommended that placement in the English program would be probably better, as it would give the child less to deal with: "she would be able to get more practice hearing the sounds that she's actually learning to read and write. You know, because she'll get the reinforcement from English everywhere, and it'll be that much easier for her" (p. 194).

It is evident that the second language achievement of the Immersion students will be markedly affected by the development of their first language skills at the start of their second language intensive exposure. Dube (1993), in her study of Immersion withdrawal, mentions that some parents noted that their children were late learning to speak and comprehending all forms of reading and writing. These parents attributed the academic difficulties of their children in Immersion to a general language delay. Parents who see their children struggling in the Immersion program come to the realization that their children need to have their weak native language skills promoted and more firmly established before attempting the acquisition of another language.

By the same token, Sparks, Ganschow et al. (1992) derive, from their studies of at-risk foreign language learners, that students who receive direct instruction in the elements of their native language (phonology, morphology, syntax) develop not only more efficient native language skills, but also improve substantially their foreign language aptitude (p. 48). A later study by Sparks, Ganschow and Patton (1995) shows that learners with good native oral and written language skills, as well as foreign language aptitude, experience much greater success in foreign language learning. As for Lavine and Schwartz (1996), they also recommend referring to the student's first language to know how she will perform in the new language, for problems in first language grammar, syntax, diction, spelling and phonology will be exaggerated in the new language. Indeed, a strong linguistic proficiency in the mother tongue helps in developing similar academic skills in the second language and the common underlying proficiency that exists across languages makes it possible, then, for skills of one language to transfer to the other.

The question of the suitability of bilingual education resurfaces with an emphasis on poor native language proficiency. As seen earlier, it was maintained by researchers like Bruck (1982) and Genesee (1992) that switching out of French Immersion was not justified on the basis of two main reasons: 1) The poor academic results remain unchanged and the children experience feelings of frustration, unhappiness and low self-esteem during the year after the switch; 2) Despite their difficulties, the children can still acquire French oral communication skills (termed BICS [basic interpersonal communicative skills] by Cummins [1984]) when they stay in the Immersion program. However, they still experience difficulty in acquiring French literacy skills (termed CALP [cognitive academic language proficiency] by Cummins [1984]), and one wonders how well they are able to progress in subjects like social studies and science when lacking these more abstract skills.

To what extent should these children be pushed to learn in an unfamiliar linguistic environment? It is my experience that they often resent the extra load of learning the semantic, syntactic and grammatical structures of the new language. It increases the confusion and the misunderstanding of concepts, and as the reading material becomes more complex, children feel very frustrated at not being able to extract meaning from written texts. It is also my experience and personal opinion that the context-reduced and cognitively demanding language of the academic subjects compound and exacerbate the learning difficulties of children with poor cognitive and linguistic abilities. These children find it very hard to achieve literacy competence in Immersion because the heavy linguistic demands exceed their cognitive and linguistic development. They may achieve a certain fluency in context embedded situations at the beginning of their Immersion experience, but they are soon overwhelmed by the academic demands of the program and feel they cannot continue. The linguistic environment is not appropriate or helpful in providing the help they need to upgrade their linguistic and academic skills. They may not experience greater success in the regular program, but learning in their native tongue may give them more confidence and encourage them to try harder.

Several UNESCO declarations have focused on the various problems that education in a second language can posit for young children, especially for those with learning difficulties. The importance of educating children in their mother tongue has often been the object of these declarations.

UNESCO Declarations on First Language Education

In a 1953 report of a 1951 meeting of experts regarding vernacular languages in education, it was stated that every effort should be made to provide education in the mother tongue:

> *It is axiomatic that the best medium for teaching a child is his mother tongue. Psychologically, it is the system of meaningful signs that in his mind works automatically for expression and understanding. Sociologically, it is a means of identification among the members of the community to which he belongs. Educationally, he learns more quickly through it than through an unfamiliar linguistic medium. (p. 11)*

Young children who have not completely developed self-expression in their native language may find it quite difficult to express themselves through the new vocabulary and syntax. Transferring ideas from one language to another is at best not an easy process. Thus, children who do not completely know their own language before learning another one may experience a great deal of frustration and difficulty in eventually achieving an adequate level of self-expression. A tense situation is also created when school communications, which are of a different nature from the home communications, are made in an unfamiliar language. Consequently, their progress can be expected to slow down. Moreover, children who are experiencing learning difficulties will not be able to get help from their parents. It is with these objections in mind that the report recommends that "the use of the mother tongue be extended to as late a stage in education as possible" (p. 48) for the simple reason that it is the best medium for effectively teaching a child.

The report also rejects the claim of a better acquisition of a second language when it is used as the medium of instruction:

> *However, recent experience in many places proves that an equal or better command of the second language can be imparted if the school begins with the mother tongue as the medium of instruction, subsequently introducing the second language as a subject of instruction. (p. 49)*

What is more, this second language should be introduced gradually and the transition to its use as a medium of instruction should also be done gradually.

Another subsequent report by Poth (1980) deals with psycho-pedagogical principles and warns against not taking heed of the expression ability of the children in the second language. Can they express in words not only their daily preoccupations, but also their feelings, their notions of space and time as well as their reasoning and conceptualization powers?

> *If the child is unexpectedly deprived of the linguistic medium to which he is accustomed, and if a new instrument of expression is imposed on him which he cannot handle and by which he is disconcerted, he is reduced to the external acquisition of no more than a few mere rudiments, too scant and too incoherent in their functioning to permit him to master reflective thought. (p. 40)*

If the new means of instruction is not mastered well enough to permit proper understanding of technical or academic subjects (which is the case for children with learning difficulties), then, no benefit will be derived from the teaching provided. Failure to determine the child's ability prior to the introduction of those school subjects "would mean relying more on haphazard groping and trial and error instead of basing educational theory and method firmly on knowledge of the child and of his capabilities" (p. 18). Poth's (1988) report adds that teaching children in a language they do not yet know requires a double effort from them:

If we have recourse to a foreign language to convey syllabus content we are requiring a double effort from children who have just started school. They must interpret a message imparted in a language they do not yet know and at the same time master the content of that message. The difficulties are therefore both of substance and of form. (p. 23)

This new linguistic form also demands a greater amount of effort and energy that could be better used learning other things.

When children possess only a rudimentary knowledge of the language of instruction, they find themselves in a school environment that is totally not adapted to their basic needs and certainly not conducive to learning. Furthermore, the foreign language cannot replace the mother tongue in the acquisition of early learning or the development of abstract intelligence. In the first school years, the child's foreign language functional level is too low to permit proper assimilation of knowledge. The consequences, therefore, are far reaching for the at-risk child, affecting the build up of her spirit and the development of her maturity.

Genetic or Environmental Conditions?

First and second language proficiencies are significantly correlated as they develop from a common underlying language learning capacity (Cummins, 1978). But does the concept of language learning capacity, and for that matter foreign language aptitude, imply irreversible conditioning? Not everyone would readily adopt such a theoretical outlook on first language acquisition or second language learning.

Skehan (1989) finds that the foreign language aptitude-achievement relationship connects more to a set of variables like the social class, the vocabulary development of the learners and their parents' education than to their language aptitude per se. Carroll (1981) also agrees that an individual's foreign language aptitude is crucially dependent upon her past learning experiences. These experiences bear the strong influence of the individual's socio-economic background. However, he reflects: "Yet, what evidence I have suggests that foreign language aptitude is *relatively* fixed over long periods of an individual's life span and relatively hard to modify in any significant way" (p. 86). Skehan (1989), referring to the follow up research to the Bristol Language Project, reaches a similar conclusion in regards to language aptitude stability over the years.

Shore (1995) claims that although no behavior genetics studies have so far differentiated between genetic versus environmental contributions to language style, variability in rate of communicative development and syntactic sophistication have been related to genetic factors.[2] As well, Pinker (1994) infers from studies of language impaired individuals that:

> *there must be some pattern of genetically guided events in the development in the brain...that is specialized for the wiring in of linguistic computation. And these construction sites seem to involve circuitry necessary for the processing of grammar in the mind, not just the articulation of speech sounds by the mouth or the perception of speech sounds by the ear. (p. 324)*

The lasting deficit for the language impaired individuals of these studies involve mostly grammar, and so Pinker (1994) concludes: "So for now there is suggestive evidence for grammar genes, in the sense of genes whose effects seem most specific to the development of the circuits underlying parts of grammar" (p. 325).

The Linguistic Coding Differences Hypothesis

In 1991, Sparks and Ganschow introduced the Linguistic Coding Differences Hypothesis (LCDH) into the foreign language literature. The LCDH attempts to explain foreign language learning difficulties. While it assumes that the innate ability to acquire language varies from individual to individual, it emphasizes the importance of the phonological/orthographic skill in language learning. It proposes that skills in the native language components, phonological, orthographic, syntactic and semantic, provide the basic foundation for learning a second language; developmental difficulties (subtle or overt) in any of these language skills will likely have a negative impact on both the native and second language systems: "difficulties in an individual's understanding of or inability to use the language codes are a likely cause of FL learning difficulties" (1993, p. 290). Sparks and Ganschow (1995) speculate that the students with phonological/orthographic processing difficulties are able to develop compensatory strategies to remediate their problems. They experience success in school, but their strategies become less efficient when confronted with an unfamiliar linguistic code; their specific difficulties "reemerge when learning the new sound-symbol system of a foreign language"[3] (p. 639). Levine (1987) follows the same line of thinking when he states: "For many students who are struggling academically, the addition of a foreign language in eighth or ninth grade is the proverbial straw that breaks the camel's back" (p. 382).

This connection between both native and second language processing abilities is based mainly, according to Sparks and Ganschow (1993), on the phonological processing ability of the learner in oral and written language. These authors claim that the fault for the learning difficulties in second language lie with an "inefficiently functioning phonetic module"[4] (p. 295). They assume the cognitive weakness is modular because: "if it were not, the deficient module would depress the student's overall cognitive functioning, causing language learning difficulties in many areas" (p. 292). This particular phonetic module, highly specific to the learning of the sound system of the language and specialized for speech processing and production, causes subtle or overt difficulties with the oral and written aspects of one's native language when it operates inefficiently. (The interrelation between the oral and the written components of language being very complex, the efficiency of the oral language seems to affect the performance of the written language and vice versa [Johnson, 1993]). This in turn affects the listening to and speaking and writing of a second language. Finally, perception and production in the second language may be poor enough to affect understanding of both oral and written words.

Limited phonological awareness and ability to encode or decode the oral and written word, then, may very well be one of the underlying factors interfering with the ability to learn a second language efficiently; the elements that go into the learning of a first language not only appear to play a significant role in the acquisition of a second language, but they may also be at the root of the individual differences observed in second language acquisition. In other words, the kinds of second language problems encountered by learners are similar to those encountered in their native language and are linked to poor sound-symbol relations (auditory ability), poor memory of words and recognition of rules governing their structures and meanings (Levine, 1987). "A student with a language disorder in his/her own language can find it especially hard to learn a foreign language. So, some kids who have even very mild language problems in English get into real difficulty when they have to take a second language" (Levine, 1990, p. 98).

MacIntyre (1995) suggests that the LCDH hypothesis is incomplete because it does not give any consideration or role to the language learning strategies as explanation of the individual foreign language learning differences. Sparks and Ganschow (1995) defend their point by stating that "most poor FL learners exhibit differences specifically related to the domain of language" (p. 238) and that training the learners into adopting learning strategies would not remediate the weakness of the phonological module; this inefficient module does not disrupt the operation of central processes as the overall cognitive ability of the learner is relatively not affected. In other words, inefficient second language learning strategies derive more from a specific cognitive weakness such as phonological processing.

However, while phonetic encoding is certainly essential to efficient second language acquisition, it is far from being sufficient. What happens in the case of an unmotivated learner with high aptitude? Do the learning difficulties just reflect a matter of general dislike toward school or more precisely a total lack of interest toward language learning? Another case scenario is that of a language learner who decides to quit the second language program despite being successful in it. For instance, a student of mine, Lynn, was fairly successful in the Immersion program. She quit at the end of Grade 11, not because of any dissatisfaction with the program, but mainly because she had lost interest. She was pursuing a career in volleyball and practice time for that sport had become a priority. Craig is another student who switched out of the Immersion program in Grade 11. When he visited me at lunch time, I asked him if he missed his Immersion classes: "Heavens, no," he said, "I am glad this load is off my back. The language had become too difficult and I could not juggle my studies and my singing practice any more. I love to sing. That is my life." (Craig belongs to a famous adult choir that travels across Canada). Other students who had left the French Immersion program because of language difficulties had gone on to win the English district speech contest or had managed to gain recognition in the journalism class. The school prided itself on these accomplishments and so did the local town newspaper, where these students' articles were published week after week.

So, why did these latter students drop out of the program? Did they eventually experience difficulties with the second language because perhaps they also suffered from a deficient phonological processing ability (to a lesser degree, probably, and mild enough to affect the second language only)? Perhaps, the textbook material had become too decontextualized. Perhaps also, they had reached a level of saturation and/or disinterest in the language. Perhaps again, some students' abandonment of the commitment to learn French was due either to a dislike of hard work[5] or to the fact that they had committed themselves to other goals.

MacIntyre (1995) maintains that one variable (linguistic coding differences) could not possibly account for the individual differences in language achievement; the concept of native language coding differences cannot be the only alternative to affective explanations for failure to learn a foreign language; "phonetic coding impairment is not the best place to look for the cause of the language learning difficulty....one's full potential as a language learner is partially determined by affective variables" which represent "possible causes of individual differences in language achievement" (p. 96). There is a wide range of potential influences and "the relation between anxiety, cognition, and behavior demonstrates that emotions in general, and anxiety in particular, can and do affect cognitive processing" (p. 246). The issue is not to determine which came first: the native language difference or the affective difference which impacts the results of language learning, but rather take into consideration the interacting influences of the very unique situation each learner is facing when experiencing difficulties in learning a second language. This should help in fully understanding the processus that is taking place:

> *Explanations based on native language coding differences and those based on affective factors are best seen as supplemental to one another because, even if encoding is performed by a separate module, phonetic coding is part of a larger, integrated, cognitive and emotional system. (MacIntyre, 1995, p. 247)*

Affective variables, intrinsic or extrinsic, cover a wide range of disparate behaviors, motivations and reactions. They can represent the characteristics the learner brings to the learning experience. They depict the language learner's personality and potential, and hint at his intrinsic needs. In a study of transfer students, Campbell (1992) remarked that parents "are not faulting the French Immersion program as *it cannot meet the needs of all learners* (my emphasis) when optional programs and schools exist" (p. 216).

Chapter VIII:
Affect, Emotion and Learning

In second language learning research, much attention has been given to learning styles and strategies, as well as to the influence of anxiety, motivation, attitude and IQ factors. In the realm of second language acquisition, the focus has been on cognitive processes, whereas other issues in language learning have not been explored very much. However, more and more, scientists stress the importance of interdisciplinary research. Jacobs and Schumann (1992) suggest that "language acquisition researchers must begin to incorporate a degree of neuro-biological reality into their perception of the language acquisition process," because "different perspectives motivate researchers to explore different aspects of the same phenomenon and can lead researchers to different conclusions" (p. 295).

Consequently, this chapter examines second language learning difficulties from a totally different perspective. This chapter focuses on learners' personal and emotional needs, which play a very influential role in developing effective attitudes toward learning a second language. Unfortunately, as Toates (1988) remarks: "attempts to integrate the fields of motivation and emotion are conspicuously missing in textbooks" (p. 3). Nevertheless, I hope to show that affect, emotion and personality are intimately intertwined with the cognitive processes of learners and they represent a major force to be reckoned with; a force just as powerful as the physiological and biological limitations seen earlier. Also in this chapter, the perception of intelligence and motivation takes a new direction. They are linked to the internal dynamics of the second language student, to his potential and to his needs, which are viewed in terms of intrinsic aspiration.

The Nature of Emotions

Birbaumer and Öhman (1993) state: "Phenomenologically, emotion *is* experience" (p. 6). Emotions represent subjective experiences and are related to events that somehow induce feeling and judging in the individual; they influence how eventually this individual will think about particular situations, react to them or toward persons encountered in those situations. Emotions thus direct and focus the individual's attention in a very specific and subjective manner. They can either propel an individual toward something she appraises as good and beneficial or pull her away from what she judges to be bad and harmful:

> *Emotion links the person to his body and to his outside world. Thus, it provides a bridge to inner needs and wishes, and practically all psychological activity occurs in the context of avoiding some things or events or approaching others. (Birbaumer & Öhman, 1993, p. 3)*

Emotions create attraction or withdrawal and are felt consciously at both cognitive and physiological levels. Damasio (1994) concurs with Birbaumer and Öhman (1993) in seeing the body attentively minded by feelings (p. 159), for emotions give meaning to every aspect of human life, to perceptions, thoughts, decisions and actions.

Emotions or feelings are not a luxury; they are not to be reduced to primitive functions or "the mindless workings of biological hardware" (LeDoux, 1996, p. 115); they are very real experientially and should not be discarded for lack of objective evidence or measurement. Damasio (1994) asserts:

> *They serve as internal guides, and they help us communicate to others signals that can also guide them....Contrary to traditional scientific opinion, feelings are just as cognitive as other percepts. They are the result of a most curious physiological arrangement that has turned the brain into the body's captive audience. (p. xv)*

Emotions and Cognition

The field of cognitive science is gradually recognizing the essential role of feeling in thinking (Goleman, 1995). Schumann (1994) mentions that "from a neural perspective, affect is an integral part of cognition" (p. 232). Affect and cognition are distinguishable but inseparable, and interact without subordinating each other:

> *Thus, if one decides to analyze perception, attention, or memory mechanisms in SLA (second language acquisition) independently of affective mechanisms, one is making a large simplifying assumption....Thus, experimental results that show differences in cognition may in fact represent differences in affective modulation of these*

processes. (p. 241)

According to Damasio (1994), feelings and emotions should not be left out of any overall concept of mind (p. 158). They have "a say on how the rest of the brain and cognition go about their business" (p. 160). In other words, body and brain are indissociable, which would explain why in a learning process, the emotional system of the learner affects what he perceives, decides to focus on and eventually remembers and acquires as lasting knowledge (Schumann, 1994). Consequently, learning takes place when one wants to learn.

In a similar vein, Krashen (1981) developed the construct of the *"affective filter"* which operates on variables that characterize the identity of the learner. Schumann (1994) describes the operation of the filter in the following way:

> *When motivation is lacking, anxiety is high, and self-esteem is low, the filter is up and input will not become intake (i.e., input will not be processed so as to produce learning). When motivation and self-confidence are high, and anxiety is low, the filter will be down and the relevant input will be acquired. (p. 232)*

In other words, affect influences cognition "to promote or inhibit second language acquisition" (p. 231).

Goleman (1995) thinks that how we perform in life is determined by both IQ and emotional intelligence: "intellect cannot work at its best without emotional intelligence....When these partners interact well, emotional intelligence rises – as does intellectual ability" (p. 28). On the other hand, emotional distress exerts a devastating impact on mental clarity; it overwhelms concentration, "continually sabotaging attempts to pay attention to whatever other task is at hand" (p. 79). One cannot separate mood from attention, says Mayberg (1999) who, with other members of her team, has discovered that the brain becomes less smart when it is in a sad or depressed state.[1] Depressed people experience difficulty concentrating even on ordinary tasks.

Emotions and Reason

If emotions can nurture interests or breed dislikes, can we really trust them as a way of knowing what is around us? Does their subjective nature simply tell us more about our inner state than about our environment? Can individuals be held responsible for their emotions? So many questions with no readily forthcoming answer, for it is difficult to judge whether the environment is assessed through the emotions or if on the other hand, the latter are environment-generated. Averill (1980) says: "Stated more formally, emotions are something that happen to us (passions), not something we deliberately do (actions)" (p. 38). Later, he proposes: "Emotions come into being only through the interaction of biological and socio-cultural systems" (p. 58). So do emotions necessarily threaten rationality? Do they disrupt rather than collaborate with rational activity? Greenspan (1980) does not think so: "Indeed, the fact that emotions resist control may be part of the reason why they are useful to us, and hence in our sense rational" (p. 242). They serve a purpose, they are not so illogical. Damasio (1994) concurs: "The organism has some reasons that reason must utilize" (p. 200). LeDoux (1996) is also of the opinion that emotion and reason should not be separated, for "minds without emotions are not really minds at all. They are souls on ice" (p. 25). We cannot study one without the other, for emotion is just a kind of cognition (LeDoux, 1996).

Naturally, this does not mean that feelings cannot or should not be controlled, should they interfere with the betterment of self and society or should they promote intolerance, lawlessness, selfishness and disregard for others around. However, emotions are part of cognitive processes such as attention, perception and memory and can become "powerful motivators of future behaviors" (LeDoux, 1996, p. 19).

Emotions, Motivation and Choices

> *The key to achievement is motivation. No matter how much ability you have, no matter what kind of family you come from, no matter where you live, where you go to school or where you work, you'll never achieve anything unless you are motivated. (Mandel & Marcus, 1995, p. 17)*

In chapter VI, motivation was deemed of primordial importance; yet, it was not found to be a guarantee of successful second language learning. But do we really understand the concept of motivation and how it relates to emotion? Mandel and Marcus (1995) propose a strict recipe of four essential ingredients for motivation: "vision, commitment, planning and follow through" (p. 17). They add: "Every ingredient is very important and must be followed in the correct order along the way while putting together this simple but unalterable recipe" (p. 8). A vision or a goal reflects an individual's values and beliefs; it implies choices, initiative and determination. Keller (1983) defines motivation as "the choices people make as to what experiences or goals they will approach or avoid, and the degree of effort they will exert in that respect" (p. 389).

There is a great deal to be learnt from the students' various likes and dislikes. When sharing their aspirations with the teacher, they unknowingly divulge where the learning obstacles might originate from; one clearly discerns internal dynamic factors which engender a very personal perception of the value of time and energy spent in the activity of learning a second language. The latter requires intrinsic motivation, a personal conviction steeply rooted in the affective domain of the individual. Ehrman (1996) thinks that people "tend to put their cognitive and emotional resources where their interests and values are" (p. 139). Williams and Burden (1997) echo the same opinion regarding intrinsic motivation, which they suggest is "best illustrated by the enormous range of obsessional interests that capture the hearts and minds of different people" (p. 125). This statement struck a very sensitive cord in my heart.

A few years ago, my daughter was admitted to a prestigious Canadian university at the age of 16. Scientifically minded, she always had had the desire to pursue a career in medicine. To be more precise, she had elected to become a heart surgeon. All through her high school years, she had shown incredible interest and diligence in the presentation of all kinds of scientific projects and had participated in several science fairs where she had won distinction and recognition. There was no doubt in our minds that she was destined to lead the life of a scientist. At the end of her third year of Biochemistry, she thought she had made a mistake and was following the wrong path. In a state of utter confusion, we urged her to continue and hoped that this sudden and unexpected change of heart would quickly reverse itself. Unfortunately, this was the first perceptible sign of a more permanent situation to come. At the end of the four-year degree, our daughter announced that she had definitively and finally found her true calling in life; she had discovered her real vocation; it was not in medicine; it was in the performing art of dancing!

I will let you guess the extent of our shock and disappointment as parents. A mini state of emergency was declared in the household as we both suffered reactions that resembled cardiac arrest (no pun intended). Who could have predicted that the dancing lessons of the primary years had marked our daughter for life, and sown in her a seed of such formidable potency that it would propel her to abandon medical studies for dancing shoes? We felt certain she was chasing a dream that would lead nowhere.

I can sense the reader is curious to find out how the story further unfolds: after a great deal of practice and perseverance she was accepted at the Toronto School of Dancing, where she completed a degree in dancing and choreography. She then found unsurpassed happiness on the stages of New York. These events had a profound effect on my thinking. I came to the conclusion that the success of a life is not to be measured in terms of financial rewards (a life of penury in this case), but rather in terms of satisfaction of heart and mind – of an inner peace so soothing to the soul. On a similar note of spurned financial rewards, passionate aspirations and treasured satisfaction of heart and mind, Yanni, a worldwide renowned musician,[2] once declared: "I have done my music the way I wanted to do it. I was willing to starve and be an unknown for the rest of my life, to do what I wanted to do."

Very often, life provides particular experiences destined to instill in some of us the wisdom that the understanding of specific problems requires. This experience of my own daughter travelling along the path of her destiny – in dancing shoes – sent me many a time into deep reflections. It helped me to recognize the innate nature of the individual, a nature that would neither comply with someone else's agenda, nor could it comply with it, because like each seed is destined to produce a certain plant and not another, so is each individual destined to answer the call of his true nature and vocation (Hillman, 1996). Born to dance? "I was born to sing….I'm driven by I don't know what….You must live off your own instincts" says the famous diva, Dame Kiri Te Kanawa.[3] As for Sartre,[4] the certitude of his vocation as a writer was all too evident to him: "I existed only in order to write" (p. 153), "if I go a day without writing, the scar burns me" (p. 164), "I had the bump of literature; therefore I would write, I would work that vein all my life" (p. 165). On the same subject of vision, life obsession and mission, Ratey and Johnson (1997) write:

> *the single most critical improvement anyone can make in brain function, and in character, is to find his mission in life. Passion heals; a whole-hearted commitment to a calling, or a career, or an avocation focuses the mind and the soul. (p. 363)*

The emotional personalities of people play a crucial role in the choices they make in life. These choices reflect their needs; they bring them satisfaction and fulfillment. What really matters, finally, is passion, "which may be more predictive of capacity and productive of motivation than other usual benchmarks" (Hillman, 1996, p. 160). Williams and Burden (1997) declare:

> *"An individual's decision to act will be influenced by internal factors. The extent to which such factors interact with each other and the relative importance that individuals attribute to them will affect the level and extent of learner's motivation to complete a task or maintain activity" (p. 137).*

In one of his lectures given in Stuttgart in 1919, Rudolf Steiner, well-known for his thoughts on education, declared: "A feeling is very closely related to will" (p. 57) and a child may have "special powers in the region of the will" (p. 89). One has to try to understand the real nature of the child. A child who lacks motivation and displays an uncooperative attitude towards his studies may very well have a "will" that is "asleep" (p. 89).

Williams and Burden (1997) construe motivation as: "a state of cognitive and emotional arousal, which leads to a conscious decision to act, and which gives rise to a period of sustained intellectual and/or physical effort in order to attain a previously set goal (or goals)" (p. 120). Likewise, motivation in language learning requires the learner to consciously choose to participate actively in the learning process; a motivated learner will show persistence, concentration, attention and effort when engaging in activities generated by the learning situation. But efficient learning can only take place when what is to be learnt is seen as being personally relevant to the learner. Learning that involves the whole being emotionally and cognitively is very likely to last and infuse a feeling of satisfaction and accomplishment. Motivation of this sort will arise, naturally, when the learning situation meets the learner's important personal needs, vision or goal. On the other hand, this type of motivation cannot arise when the learner is forced by outside pressure to participate in a learning situation that bears no relevance to her personal needs and or does not arouse her curiosity or interest.

Emotions and Successful Learning

"It is generally accepted that human motives to engage in a particular activity are based on underlying needs" (van Els, Bongaerts et al. 1984, p. 116). Individuals like to be successful and will choose activities in which they feel they can experience success – activities they are probably predisposed to carry out – activities which they find rewarding, useful and meaningful to themselves. Choosing these activities necessarily requires knowledge of one's own psychological nature, for this psychological nature reflects the emotional needs, the goals, the desires and the instincts of the individual (Myklebust, 1994).

Kuhl and Karzen-Saad (1988) state that "Many behavioral and emotional disorders seem to be based on errors of motivation, that is, on the fact that individuals do not behave according to their own motivational preferences" (p. 66). The relationship between motivation and emotion can serve learning in either a positive or negative manner. Learners can regress in motivation and performance if their requirements for emotional security are not met (Kuhl and Karzen-Saad, 1988). But, by engaging in the action of learning with intrinsic motivation, "a sense of volition" or "a sense of unpressured willingness" (Deci, Ryan & Williams, 1996, p. 165), learners experience autonomy and enjoy a conflict-free learning situation. This contributes greatly to the learning process; it gives the students the energy and the drive to better internalize the material of the learning situation. Moreover, "people develop enduring interest in activities at which they feel self-efficacious and from which they derive self-satisfaction" (Bandura, 1988, p. 51); but, as well, people choose activities and set goals which not only reflect their orientations and interests, but which create harmony and emotional stability. Goleman (1995) finds that high-achieving students enjoy studying, experience an "absorbing challenge of flow" (p. 94), whereas low-achieving students do little studying and spend more time socializing. Learners who experience joy and self-determination in the act of learning also experience their behavior as an expression of themselves (Deci, Ryan & Williams, 1996).

In Immersion there is evidence of this kind of behavior among students who find personal satisfaction and value in learning a second language and therefore are in possession of a powerful force that Mandel and Marcus (1995) call "commitment" (p. 19). On the other hand, a mismatch between motivation and enjoyment or emotion will obstruct progress and lead to some kind of negative action, because emotions represent a way of responding to pressures. Indeed, they indicate that a situation has arisen that is disruptive and irrational to the individual.

Emotions Ignored

Learners who experience difficulties find that the acquisition of a second language brings about a conflict between two linguistic codes (that of their mother tongue and that of the second language).

> *Language is composed of symbols that are abstract and often hard to pin down. Concepts and expressions in any two languages do not relate one-to-one....Thick ego boundaries...may interfere...so that a learner...does not even become conscious of the new information, or becomes aware of it in only a very superficial way. (Ehrman, 1996, p. 120)*

A lack of success in learning a second language, whether it be due to a learning disability or a lack of goal or commitment, can trigger self-esteem problems as well as feelings of insecurity and anxiety which in turn, further interfere with learning. Sometimes, unsuccessful students view such a situation as "a threat to the perceived integrity" (Ehrman, 1996, p. 138) of their own identity and competence. Also, when students' personal needs are not being met or when their personal goals are being ignored and blocked, frustration sets in; it can eventually lead to hostility and aggression. "Sometimes the feelings are a smoke screen for something else: In every case, though, they constitute an important signpost to what is going on with the learner" (Ehrman, 1996, p 137).

It is my personal experience that students who are angry, or feel uncomfortable and anxious over school assignments they cannot do, will easily see in their parents and teachers the source of their discomfort; they blame these adults who force them to work at a subject they resent – a subject which prevents them from attending to their desires and goals, from nurturing the beliefs they have about themselves and their potential. The anger that arises from this environmental interference can energize aggressive behavior which will target others: parents and teachers; sometimes the students will turn to self-aggression or redirect their aggression against another object as well. Myklebust (1994) describes very well the pattern followed by the onset of anger due to:

feeling unable to live up to what is expected; which in turn, leads to expressing anger and aggressiveness [trying to fight back]; finally followed by guilt, shame, remorse, sadness, despair, and depression. This sequence leads to more feelings of inadequacy, so the cycle of emotional conflict continues – an extremely debilitating chain of events. (p. 60)

According to Hoffman (1983), the interplay between the child's central auditory processing disorder and resulting learning disability creates subsequent negative emotional correlates such as frustration, anxiety, stress and aggressiveness (p. 320). The emotional trauma undermines the child's emotional stability and internal control. The restlessness that follows further reduces the ability to function in the classroom, for every individual will attempt to deal or cope with the emotions and their source in one way or another. There is definitely resistance to learning and in some extreme cases, one could witness depression, school phobia or a "fearful withdrawal from threatening situations" (Hoffman, 1983, p. 321).

All these negative behaviors and emotional responses (withdrawal, tantrums, refusal to follow directions, avoidance of school and homework, conflict between parent and child) were symptomatic of some of the Immersion students described in chapter I. These defense mechanisms and expressions of frustration are so many ways that learners in difficulty adopt to cope with an unpleasant situation and express their unhappiness (or mask their learning disability); they are also "defensive of emotional equilibrium and self-esteem" (Ehrman, 1996, p. 147).

Weininger, interviewed by Nicolson (*Today's Parent*, February 1989) "feels that a disproportionate number of the troubled children he sees in a psycho-educational clinic at OISE come from French immersion programmes. 'The problems aren't just lack of academic success – they're also related to aggression and withdrawal'" (p. 32). It must be noted at this point that students with learning difficulties do not necessarily use their emotions to correct the unsuitable conditions. Sometimes, the emotions are inhibited and do not manifest themselves in hostile behavior. The sadness of a student, as seen in chapter I, can be conveyed by his passive and apathetic demeanor. Another reaction of students experiencing learning difficulties is to disown the problem and the responsibility of their behavior, especially when they perceive others (parents, educators, society) are controlling and forcefully imposing upon them goals that do not correspond to "their own construction of the world.... their internal attributes....their personality" (Williams & Burden, 1997, p. 137), or their "uniqueness and destiny" (Hillman, 1996, p. 14).

Emotions open a window on what goes on within the individual. For the students struggling in the Immersion program, the emotive reactions and expressions of frustration represent a gauge of the inner state of the individual – of the intense inner conflict that suffocates; they are an attempt to change the world around them and lift the burdensome performance imposed upon them; they are a means of communicating the difficulties that have become too great to handle. Emotions also permit the surrounding community to become aware of the needs and capabilities of the "sufferer" and to re-evaluate the expectations against the reality of her world and the reality of her personality (Averill, 1980). Indeed, children who are given tasks beyond their capacities soon "lose confidence, enthusiasm...and interest in succeeding at school" (Greenspan, 1997, p. 213). Unfortunately, the signs of distress are often ignored. Many times educational choices are made "irrespective of the child's particular learning characteristics" (Trites & Moretti, 1986, p. 16).

Day and Shapson (1983) indicate that even when students' learning problems are evident, and the learning assistant teacher and the psychologist have advised transfer, some principals accept this transfer "with much reluctance and only in rare circumstances" (p. 17). In one instance, the school policy subscribed to the notion that (learning difficulties and emotional problems or not), "when a commitment is made, the home and school must encourage children to persevere" (p. 17). Bonyun, Morrison and Unitt (1986) mention that in some cases, parents themselves do not wish to have their child transfer out of Immersion even when this appears to be a solution to their child's learning difficulties. These authors also report that some principals resist the attitude that a child who has a problem should drop out of the program.

Stern (1991) finds that in some instances children are counseled to stay in Immersion despite the problems and the stress they experience because leaving the program would be "like a demotion" (p. 170). The logic for keeping these children in French is simple: the "slight extra stress" (p. 170) is compensated by the fact that these children have friends in the program. Some parents also indicate that their child will not be moved out of the program despite the psychologist's recommendation of transfer due to academic weaknesses. Campbell (1992) relates how some parents are encouraged to keep their children in the program even though they are experiencing difficulties; they are convinced by some teachers and principals not to switch their children out of Immersion on the basis of the validity of the program and of the anticipation of a change in the children's attitude and motivation. It is believed in these cases that parents and children "need to live out the unmotivated stage" (p. 186). Dube (1993) remarks that although "educators are concerned with the academic and emotional aspect of the children who are experiencing difficulty in French immersion" (p. 4), parents are encouraged to keep their children in Immersion despite the difficulty.

Thomas and Chess (1984) talk of "goodness of fit," a consonance between the individual and the environment (p. 1). There is goodness of fit when the individuals' capacities, motivations and behavior are in agreement with the expectations and demands of the environment or the learning situation. On the other hand, there is "dissonance" (p. 8) when a poor relationship exists between the individuals and their environment "so that distorted development and maladaptive functioning occur" (p. 8). According to these authors, disturbed behavioral functioning is not due to the demands, stresses and conflicts which are in keeping with the child's developmental potentials and capacities, but rather to "excessive stress resulting from poorness of fit between environmental expectations and demands and the capacities of the child at a particular level of development" (p. 8). What is more, failure to recognize the symptoms of emotional maladjustment, even though the child may seem to accept the learning conditions and comply dutifully with his parents' wishes and expectations, may create a more unbearable situation later on. Myklebust (1994) explains that "Compromises with our feelings, with our conscience, with our values, can be deeply disturbing. Sometimes the price we pay for compromise might be the last straw and cause us psychological and physical pain" (p. 27). Depression can be such a price to pay and a very high price indeed, as "even the mildest of depressions, silences the soul" (Ratey & Johnson, 1997, p. 103).

Chapter IX:
Personal Needs, Goals and Education

The powerful role that affect and emotions exert on cognition, motivation and choices has been examined, and it was determined that to a great extent, success in second language learning (as in any learning endeavor) is very relevant to the affinity and inclination that the learner shows toward the subject. On the other hand, ignoring the emotions can affect adversely the cognitive processes of the second language learner and lead to a poorness of fit that breeds sorrow and failure. The present chapter proposes, on the strength of Gardner's (1985) *Multiple Intelligences*, to assess parents' expectations and review the role of education relative to the needs, goals and natural abilities of the children. I will also attempt to show that within a humanistic framework of education, there is no place for elitism.

Parents' Expectations

Expectations of a better access to jobs and a higher socio-economic level represent a major part of parents' reasons for enrolling their children in Immersion. These expectations sometimes seem to take precedence over their children's well-being, aptitude and interests. Can this parental driving force ever infuse in all Immersion children enough motivation and enthusiasm to follow their parents' agenda? On the other hand, isn't there a possibility that some children, especially those with learning difficulties, may want to direct their energy toward different goals?

However, parents' choice of the Immersion program seems "to reflect more a 'life-style' decision" (Trites, Moretti, 1986, p. 16). Both Lebrun (1988) and Bibeau (1991) observe that Immersion programs seem to give very little consideration to the children's individual needs; instead these programs appear to cater more to the parents' expectations and objectives, to their wishes of esteemed positions for their children in the Canadian societal structure. Campbell (1992) also remarks that "The social, political, economic and cultural implications of the immersion philosophy tend to over-ride the significance of the needs of the child in the immersion program" (p. 39).

Parents who put pressure on their children to remain in a program which they do not enjoy and in which they find neither satisfaction nor success, may nonetheless see their children graduate in that program; however, the program demands and the parents' expectations of scholastic achievement may be so unrealistic in light of the children's talents and interests, that these children's progress in other school subjects may be impeded as well.

I have learned from personal experience that parents need to remember that children are not an extension of themselves; they are individuals with their own interests, likes and dislikes; they cannot fulfill or gratify their parents' own needs. If children do badly in school, parents must not feel that this is a reflection of their parenting skills either; there are no real failures, but only experiences that should be perceived as a way of better understanding the individuals' immediate needs. As well, having and keeping a child in Immersion should not be considered a status symbol.

Differences in Human Nature

Although, we should all experience similar success in learning language, Bialystok and Hakuta (1994) remark that "it seems undeniable that some people find it easier to learn a second language than do others" (p. 125). The underpinnings of second language learning ability and motivation include the interplay of many personal, individual-difference factors that cannot always be explained adequately. One of these factors is the influence of biology, which I believe has been given little consideration in the world of Immersion; not only should biology and one's own inherent limitations, talents and or needs be given their proper place, but one should not be reluctant to consider biological explanations of success or potential.

Kagan (1994) talks of "an inherited neuro-chemical and physiological profile that is linked to emotion and behavior" (p. 33). This profile emerges early in life and creates a particular temperament that contributes greatly to the personality of the individual. Consequently, according to Kagan (1994), the development of talent or specific abilities is not just a matter of will, and we cannot blame children who, "despite effort, have difficulty learning to read rapidly or to dance with grace. We acknowledge that these qualities lie outside of will" (p. 297). Likewise, learning a second language does not depend only upon the individual's will or wish.

Each child's personality is unique, for "the biological givens of his brain" (Ratey & Johnson, 1997, p. 17) dictate how he attends to his outer surroundings and reacts to the multiple everyday experiences. Each child, then, demonstrates a particular way of processing and integrating information. Greenspan (1997) concurs with these authors in claiming that children "enter the world with widely varied potentials and predilections....They diverge neurologically and physiologically....Each child therefore proceeds through the developmental stages at his or her own pace, finding some tasks more and others less difficult" (p. 217). Parents themselves often insist that each of their children is a distinct individual; consequently, no method of upbringing or education can possibly suit all children.

Kinds of Intelligences

We have seen that IQ was not found to be an essential factor of achievement in second language learning. But what is intelligence? Can it be fairly evaluated, objectively assessed? Can it be viewed in terms other than measurements produced by more or less sophisticated instruments or tests?

Gardner (1985) mentions that there is, coming from the neurology discipline, increasingly persuasive evidence of units in the nervous system (p. 57). Today, intelligence is no longer considered a uniform cognitive capacity. Gardner proposes an alternative explanation based on a different view of the mind. According to his theory of Multiple Intelligences, the brain is seen as being *modular* in design (see note 4 in chapter 7). "Separate psychological processes appear to be involved in dealing with linguistic, numerical, pictorial, gestural, and other kinds of symbolic systems" (Gardner & Hatch, 1989, p. 5). Gardner's theory also conceives of a person's intelligence as being made up of autonomous faculties labeled "intelligences." Gardner identified seven such faculties. One of the faculties identified by Gardner in 1983 is Linguistic Intelligence. Language is an ability developed by everyone; yet, not everyone will develop language to the same proficiency level.

Gardner explains that some individuals are endowed with the Linguistic Intelligence,[1] whereas others demonstrate "selective difficulties" (p. 84) in the learning of language. As well, Gardner emphasizes that even the plasticity in human growth during the early months of life is "modulated by strong genetic constraints which operate from the beginning and which guide development along some paths rather than along others" (p. 32). According to research, four- and five-year-old children already exhibit at this tender age "profiles of strength and weakness" (Gardner & Hatch, 1989, p. 4).

Every individual will develop different intellectual strengths.[2] Gardner (1985) also advances that individuals not only differ greatly from one another in the speed with which they develop their abilities in particular areas, but they may experience, as well, that success and speed in one area does not necessarily entail similar speed and success in other areas (p. 27):

> *I strongly challenge the notion of large general powers. To my way of thinking, the mind has the potential to deal with several different kinds of content, but an individual's facility with one content has little predictive power about his or her facility with other kinds of content. (p. xi)*

Kagan (1989) expresses a similar opinion on the concept of general intelligence as the underpinning of every kind of ability and accomplishment. He cites the example of Einstein, who failed the foreign language course in school and experienced great difficulty in learning English as a second language later. Kagan (1989) states: "I also share the popular belief...that each unusual talent requires some special biological configuration of brain structure and chemistry that favors a specific competence, be it with numbers, images, words, notes, machines, or brush and oil" (p. 207).

Mandel and Marcus (1995) echo the same conceptual view regarding the talent or power people are able to display across different areas. Only a minority of people are uniformly good at or show equal interest in everything they undertake: "As an adult, are you equally talented or indeed, interested in art, mathematics, languages, music and car mechanics? Not a chance!" (p. 10). Hillman (1996) relates examples of eminent persons who, although they possessed great abilities and expertise in some fields, were limited or totally incompetent in others.

On the other hand, Ericsson and Charnes (1994) do not believe that successful individuals have innate abilities and capacities. Their studies lead them to believe that differences between high and less accomplished performers reflect more the effect of acquired knowledge and skills that the intensity of training or practice bestows upon the individuals; in order to adapt to the demands of a well-defined field, this training must be performed through continuous and voluntary effort, attention and persistence. It still remains that what predisposes individuals to engage in such practice, and sustain this practice over a long period of time, represents major determining factors of accomplishment. Ericsson and Charnes (1994) add: "However, some of these factors, such as preferred activity level and temperament, may have a large genetic component" (p. 744).

The Role of Education

Learning a new language can be a traumatizing experience for children who feel the constraints of having to express themselves with borrowed forms; the awkward use of the forms and structures of the new language makes them feel hesitant and intellectually inferior, for when they speak this new language, they realize then that their thoughts do not match their verbal expressions (Bouton, 1974). Under such constraints as overlapping thoughts and comprehension patterns, learners' reactions can be very different and diverse, and Bouton (1974) suggests that the learners' intellectual, psychological and physical state should become a prime consideration when choosing learning conditions for these learners (p. 174). Indeed, the role of education is not just to transmit knowledge; its role is to involve "the whole person, the emotions and feelings" (Williams & Burden, 1997, p. 33). When a new language is introduced to convey syllabus content, children are required to provide a double effort to interpret both the message and its content; the difficulties that arise then for some children can create an unbearable situation.

> *By refusing to provide him [the student] with the verbal means to match his basic needs of expression and creativity, the school ends up by thwarting the growth and flowering of his intelligence and personality; it drives him to turn in upon himself and adopt an attitude of passivity. As a result, his ability to understand becomes atrophied, as*

> *do his natural inclinations to exteriorize his feelings and interests. (Poth, 1980, p.40)*

Poth (1988) describes the above situation as one of "regression and isolation" when "serious discontinuities are introduced into [*the children's*] emotional and cognitive development" (p. 23). Consequently, one must consider the emotional, psychological and intellectual growth of the child as a pedagogical issue of prime importance.

Wilkinson (1993), in a compendium on Steiner, states: "In our present state of evolution, that is, in the midst of our materialistic civilization, the essential thing for the individual is not to acquire more factual knowledge, even in the technical field, as some would advocate, *but to find himself*." (p. 37). For this to happen, we need individual-centered schools which can "withstand the current enormous pressures toward uniformity and unidimensional assessments" (Gardner, 1993, p. 11). Learners are quite different from one another and education should be sensitive to these differences, especially when a child is struggling in a language of instruction that is not his own. "Instead of ignoring them (*the differences*), and pretending that all individuals have [or ought to have] the same kinds of minds, we should instead try to ensure that everyone receive an education that maximizes his or her own intellectual potential" (p. 71). According to Greenspan (1997), one unfounded assumption behind the education system is the notion "that children of the same age can generally be taught as a homogeneous group by standardized methods" (p. 217). This is counterproductive; it hinders many children's potential. The result is that these children try to avoid the learning activities in which they are not interested or ready to participate actively and productively. This protective mechanism indicates that their individuality is being ignored, and it makes it difficult to justify any reason why these children should be pushed into learning material they are not ready for.

I believe the goal of education is to guide the student toward his destiny; essentially, it must help in developing the individual's inherent capacities and not "persuade him to follow some arbitrary direction" (Wilkinson, 1993, p. 38); it must enable students to develop as "individuals in their own right and thereby achieve self-actualization" (Williams & Burden, 1997, p. 35). Surely, this would entail a comprehensive curriculum with the right subjects introduced at the right time, constantly bearing in mind the child's nature, her capacities and her personality. But, moreover, this means that the learners must be encouraged to make their own choices in what and how they want to learn (Williams & Burden, 1997). "We should not try to graft on to the child something arbitrary. Subjects and lessons should be introduced out of the necessity of child nature" (Wilkinson, 1993, p. 42). Goleman (1995) suggests that the most important role of education is to help children discover the field where their talents will suit them best, where they will be satisfied and competent, and where they will be able to develop their creative energy and discover their inner self. This way a true personality can emerge and alienation can be averted. To ignore the natural aptitudes of children is akin to inviting psychological imbalance and silencing the inherent aspirations; it is an imposition that stifles the authentic self.

Consequently, educational choices must become rational and reflect the child's true nature; they must also change as the child changes in his bid to find himself. Parents and educators should therefore take heed of the students' behavior, emotions and feelings, for through them transpire the drives and the instincts that point to appropriate educational decisions. Myklebust (1994) mentions that " 'Authorities' tell us how to become successful at virtually anything, but their approaches are simplistic, if not contrary, to what we know about personal growth" (p. 3). The aim of education is to fulfill children's individual needs and develop the children's potentialities; it must help individuals find a balance between their needs, purposes and goals so they can develop dignity and self-worth and become fully developed human beings, as well as caring and responsible persons. Such attainment necessitates understanding the innate psychological nature of the students as well as their potentiality as human beings, for this is "a process that proceeds from inside to outside" (Myklebust, 1994, p. 169).

Thomas and Chess (1984) claim that the poorness of fit between the children and their environment must be changed to a goodness of fit in order to correct their behavior disorder. Following the identification of this poorness of fit, they recommend the implementation of strategies to review the expectations and demands that are beyond the children's capacities (p. 8), for it is important to take care of the children's interests and happiness so as to enable them to achieve self-actualization. Steiner (1919), commenting on the unco-operative attitude of a child towards his schoolwork, recommends: "if the thinking cognition in the child is destined not to appear until later, then he must be treated appropriately so that in his later life he may be able to work with active energy" (p. 89). In other words, the different forces in the child must be cultivated appropriately so as to allow a harmonious development of her personality and destiny. Along the same line of thinking, Gardner (1985) urges educators "to pay close heed to the biological and psychological proclivities of human beings" (p. 393).

These aspects of education portray a humanistic dimension – a dimension which emphasizes the development of the whole person and not just the acquisition of cognitive skills. A humanistic approach to education recognizes "the inner world of the learner" and places "the individual's thoughts, feelings and emotions at the forefront of all human development. These are aspects of the learning process that are often unjustly neglected, yet they are vitally important if we are to understand human learning in its totality" (Williams & Burden, 1994, p. 30). A humanistic approach to education implies that everyone is recognized as an individual and is helped into becoming himself as opposed to being forced to comply with the wishes of others who do not understand that personality and inner self have specific demands. It is an approach that rests on an awareness of the neurological and emotional development of the child.

Learning a second language is only one facet of education; and so, when despite concentration and hard work, success in the Immersion program remains evasive, the learners who experience difficulties may wish to invest their efforts and resources in other activities that do not undermine their perceived self-efficacy. It is then very important that learners receive help and support in matching personal capabilities with attainable goals. As seen earlier, negative discrepancies between the two can breed depressive moods, alienation and a self-perception of incompetence. Kuhl and Kazen-Saad (1988) explain: "This phenomenon occurs when subjects continue to perform a subjectively unpleasant activity....Depression is frequently accompanied by behavior that is chronically discrepant [i.e., alienated] from motivational preferences" (p. 66). Indeed, students who constantly experience difficulties with a school subject end up taking an aversion[3] to it and soon find themselves in a chronic state of emotional flurry. In terms of the Immersion program, Genesee and Hamayan (1980) advise that "caution should be exercised in making irreversible educational decisions concerning the language program options of individual students" (p. 108). Cummins (1984), who advocates the Immersion program for children with a wide range of learning abilities and language skills, nonetheless also recommends that each case of learning difficulties:

> *be judged on its individual merits....under some conditions it might be appropriate to transfer the child to an English programme. For example, if a child has been unhappy for a prolonged period of time in an immersion program and wants to switch, then it is probably right to do so. (p. 176)*

Stern (1991) recommends that guidelines be developed to "advise parents about the pros and cons" (p. 248) of the program. "Both sides of the coin" (p. 248) should be presented to the parents and not just the positive features of the program. This is so the risks as well as the benefits can be weighed carefully and an informed decision be made by parents about the suitability of French Immersion for their children. Dube (1993) reports that parents whose children experienced difficulties in Immersion recommend that you monitor the children's progress very closely and to withdraw the unhappy children struggling academically, for "Each child is different and because one child does well your other[s] might not. It's worth the effort to give it a try and know when to let go" (p. 52). Indeed, a child needs to feel successful and when she has been given extra help and is still experiencing difficulty, other parents are of the opinion that: "it would seem pointless to pursue it.... take seriously your child's concern. It's not for everyone" (p. 53).

Elitism

If on the basis of the diverse reasons given so far, Immersion is not a suitable program for all children, are we then in danger of seeing this program turning elitist? Olson and Burns (1983) note that French Immersion is better understood "*functionally* as a process of *class* identification" (p. 7). These authors explain that French Immersion children are elite not only in terms of their socio-economic background, but also in terms of the selection that happens when "problem" and "language difficulty" children are "exiled" (p. 7) from the Immersion classes: "the effect, if not the intent, has been to generate an elite cohort" (p. 7). Cummins (1984) recommends that the "push-out" (p.176) phenomenon in Immersion programs be addressed because of serious negative consequences for the society as a whole in terms of second language enrichment being reserved for an elite group of students. Genesee (1992) is of the opinion that if all the at-risk students opt out of Immersion, "a weakened, inferior 'regular' program" (p. 201) will emerge, and an elitist Immersion program with higher quality students will result from this selection. Keep (1993) writes: "There is a hidden selection process in FI which leads to a type of elitism" (p. 5). The level of attrition being as high as it is, the Immersion program must necessarily be comprised of a higher functioning group of students who remain in the program as "survivors" (p. 58). Elitism, according to Keep (1993), involves the exclusion of lower functioning students from the Immersion program.

The association of elitism with French Immersion also comes from a consistent finding that the program is mostly comprised of children from families with higher socio-economic status (Lapkin, Swain, Shapson, 1990). However, since Immersion is open to all, children from a wide range of socio-economic backgrounds enter the program and according to Lapkin, Swain and Shapson (1990), not only can these children succeed, but attrition does not appear to be "selective by SES background" (p. 650). Stern (1991) thinks that the notion of elitism associated with French Immersion stems from a selection that is effected on the basis of the unsuitability of the program for some children; the children thus selected, demonstrate lower intellectual scores, language and or learning difficulties and end up being barred from acquiring the benefits of second language development. "The professional participants are rendering French Immersion more elitist by recommending that children with certain kinds of difficulty transfer to an English program . . . . it [*Immersion*] is being depicted as more elitist since not all children who get into the program can succeed in the program" (p. 247). However, according to her research, Stern finds that "the transfer process is not a process of social selection" (p. 247). Not only does this selection not reveal any social dimension, but it derives instead from some children's lack of "suitable or legitimate behavior to be academically successful in the program" (p. 247). Also, there are "very few academic options available" (p. 248) to the children to deal with their learning difficulties. As paradoxical as it may seem, Immersion is open to everyone, but does not operate identically for everyone; yet it has not become an elitist program as enrolment is more related to the professionals' and the parents' perception of the child's potential to succeed or the child's ability to function successfully once she is in the program.

Keep (1993) admits that abundant evidence exists to substantiate the presence of "within-child" (p. 239) educational difficulties (cognitive processing skills, intelligence, co-operation, motivation, verbal reasoning, etc.). Yet, she does not believe that the student alone owns the problem; the learning environment represents another important variable which must be included in the assessment of the situation. But, as much as parental support, teacher, teaching style, classroom dynamics and management can make a difference to a child with learning difficulties, they can only very partially alleviate the problem.

Failing in school afflicts all levels of society. Eysenck (1973) states that educational attainment depends more on IQ than on social class or environment. According to this author the notion that education can offset differences in innate ability is a myth. Some people possess natural abilities to carry out complex and difficult jobs, while others feel predisposed for a different type of activities. These innate factors are very prevalent in sport, for example. What Eysenck suggests is that "merit, rather than parental wealth, or political influence, or other external and irrelevant factors" (p. 223) play a decisive role in determining and shaping the job or profession distribution in society. Eysenck (1973) adds: "Biology sets an absolute barrier to egalitarianism, in life as in sport" (p. 224). Hillman (1996) does not believe in the equality of all either:

> *What is the basis of this claim? Inequalities are there before the first breath....Since neither nurture nor nature gives equality, where do we even get the idea?...We are equal by the logic of eachness....we are unequal in every other respect – unfairly, unjustly, utterly unequal, except in the fact of each's unique genius. (p. 272)*

When considering the association of elitism with Immersion on the basis of socio-economic background, let us remember that it is not the class that determines the cognitive abilities of an individual, but rather the other way about. As far as charges of elitism resulting from a selection process that pushes out the less gifted students, let us remember also that children are not all alike and are not all suited to the same educational treatment, for different genetics, personality, ability and circumstances endow children with different capabilities:

> *Methods and aims which suit the academic child may not suit non-academic children, and to condemn them to competition and failure in a race in which they have no wish to take part in the first place is not a rational way to organize education. (Eysenck, 1973, p. 251)*

It is not reasonable to insist that children who are born different be treated as if their differences did not exist or to try to fit round pegs in square holes. On the other hand, we can all be equal in being treated equally.

Testing and Screening

Does the above statement entitle us to conclude that learning a second language depends upon the endowment of a special gift, the existence of which can be discovered by using the information from language aptitude tests? Should testing and screening be used in order to determine who is gifted enough to study a second language, and who consequently is going to be allowed into the language classroom? Despite the guidance available to parents who wish to enroll a child in primary French Immersion, Trites (1986) does not think that an assessment of readiness is feasible: "no set of variables had been validated as predictive of success or failure in the primary French immersion program" (p. 15).

Although, none of the factors traditionally thought to contribute to proficient second language learning is decisive in determining who will be successful in the endeavor, it is evident that "the gifted language learner has found the most advantageous blend" (Bialystok & Hakuta, 1994, p. 126) of personality factors, cognitive styles, aptitude, intelligence, motivation and attitude. Can this "blend" be explored and assessed by tests?

It is beyond the scope of this book to examine the different standardized instruments built for the purpose of measuring second language ability. Suffice it to say that there exists two major tests of second language aptitude: one, developed by Carroll and Sapon in 1959 and called the *Modern Language Aptitude Test* (MLAT), and the other one developed by Pimsleur in 1966 and called the *Language Aptitude Battery* (PLAB). The *Modern Language Aptitude Test*, when revised, gave in

1965 the four components related to foreign language aptitude: 1) Phonetic Coding Ability, 2) Grammatical Sensitivity, 3) Memory Abilities and 4) Inductive Language Learning Ability. It is thought that general ability in all four components serves as a good predictor of success in classroom language learning – success which is not so highly dependent upon intelligence as it is upon knowledge of language elements. An individual may not exhibit equal competence in each of the different components mentioned. For example, she might be more competent in the domain of written and expressive language than in the domain of the oral and receptive language, but generally speaking, if students experience difficulties in their native language, it will in turn exacerbate their second language learning difficulties. Nevertheless, according to Carroll (1985), a low aptitude score does not mean that a person cannot learn a second language; it simply means that it will take more time and effort for that person to accomplish a similar level of language proficiency than a person with a higher aptitude score. It may also mean that individual different cognitive and linguistic abilities require different instructional approaches.

Calvé (1983) is of the opinion that a battery of tests should become standard procedure in pretesting Early Immersion candidates so as to avoid a frustrating experience and negative attitudes towards learning French. Genesee (1983) does not think the pretesting is possible or even advisable:

> *It is my expressed opinion that there currently exists no single or simple criterion that can validly be used to decide the admissibility of individual children to Immersion programs. Such a decision should be based on multiple criteria and should probably be made only once the child's actual performance in Immersion can be judged. (p. 40)*

Keep (1993) reckons that testing would give false results because it would be based on the premise of the non-malleability of the child:

> *It is not feasible to perform testing as though skills were static....The assessment technology to achieve 100 percent accuracy in testing does not exist....screening would still unavoidably reject students who would have met with success and accept students who will not succeed." (p. 157)*

Bialystok and Hakuta (1994) also object to language aptitude testing. They do not advise selecting pupils on the basis of aptitude test scores alone, as outcomes of learning do not always match aptitude test results:

> *The question of individual differences in learners is completely con-founded with the question of differences in outcomes....Accordingly, proficiency, or success in learning a new language, has many facets....Language is far too complex a system to reveal itself through a single skill, a single experience, or a single test. (p. 158)*

Yet, for students who have difficulty listening and understanding the spoken form of a foreign language, testing may reveal that method-ologies stressing listening and speaking are not the right approach for some students of a foreign language (Javorsky, Sparks, Ganschow, 1992). From this would derive the potential of matching students' strengths with language instruction (adjusting to students' phonetic coding skills and presenting new material in a highly structured way, practicing and reviewing the morphological and syntactic rule struc-tures of the language, for instance) (Ganschow & Sparks, 1993). Ehrman (1996), also thinks that information from instruments such as MLAT "can be very helpful indeed. It can serve as a shortcut to finding out things that would otherwise take much longer to discover" (p. 199). She cautiously recommends, though, to try and obtain information from multiple sources in order to better judge the situation of a student in difficulty. Overall, the MLAT is only useful at the scoring extremes: "A very low score indicates weakness in all the factors; a very high score suggests strength in all the factors" (Ehrman, 1996, p. 207). Other fac-tors, such as individual variables of learning styles and environment as well as a multitude of other personal attributes, can form an intricate interplay of motivational attitude and language processing ability. "The learning processes need a nurturing context. A positive attitude, a con-ducive environment, rich exposure, and many other unnamed factors allow natural abilities to flourish" (Bialystok & Hakuta, 1994, p. 158). Language learning is multidimensional and no test would ever be able to determine with certainty the learning outcomes of individuals.

Conclusion

The knowledge of a second language is very useful, not only in promoting understanding between people, but also in providing better socio-economic opportunities in a bilingual country like Canada. Yet, the decision to instruct a child in a second language should entail the knowledge that some children are superior language learners, and for others, learning a language is a slow and painful process (Moeller, 1988).

The goal of the Immersion program is to promote bilingualism, but unfortunately, it cannot be assumed that everyone wants to or can become bilingual. The learning environment of the classroom may impede the language learning process for learners who would thrive and succeed in a natural environment. But above all, we need to consider the interaction of a multitude of individual variables. Personality traits, first language development and other factors at various levels (cognitive, emotional, phonological, neuro-psychological, bio-physiological) influence greatly the second language learning process and can turn the language learning situation into a very frustrating experience. Learners whose needs, goals and aspirations are antagonized by the imposition of an ill-fitting subject – a subject that does not fit well with their intrinsic self – become very unhappy, lose all incentive and can sink into depression. Fiedeorowiz (1995), a neuro-psychologist specializing in literacy and learning disabilities, claims that she sees, in her practice, children with learning disabilities who suffer from the harmful effects of Immersion; she claims these children would be better off in an English language program because they experience difficulty and failure.[1]

In this book, the concept of suitability of the French Immersion program for all children has been challenged. It has been examined from different perspectives in order to provide, as much as possible, an informed and educated view on the issue; one hopes that an increased awareness of students' variables will help parents and educators to recognize and accept that Immersion can be experienced in ways that differ very much:

> *What is an exciting new experience for one child or group of children may well be an oppressive obstacle for another....we must go beyond systematic theories about how all children do, can, or should learn a*

> *second language in order to penetrate the mysteries of early second-language learning. (Weininger, 1982, p. 22)*

The issue of the suitability of the Immersion program for every child leaves parents and educators facing very tough questions for which there are no easy or definite answers. Opinions vary according to the diversity of information and interests regarding both students' individual needs and social requirements. Consequently, a conflicting situation arises for parents and educators who consider only the good and the value of the Immersion program. However, it is my opinion that only the conflict lived by individuals involved in the program represents a true and reliable element. It is extremely important therefore to understand what is going on with Immersion learners who experience difficulties in the program. Only when we understand, can we make the right decision regarding what is best for each child – a decision which can be taken, then, without the uncomfortable feeling of uncertainty.

Nevertheless, reports on Immersion seem to hold privileged status and may be regarded as expert information. Yet, let us remember that contrary expert opinions do exist, and this only serves to demonstrate that the suitability of Immersion for all children is at best doubtful. However, many do quite well in the program and I concur with Carroll's (1987) remark: "to say that French immersion may not be appropriate for all children is not to say that it is inappropriate and should be abandoned" (p. 208); we can still strive to improve the program so as to accommodate as many children as possible. Levine (1987) suggests that a language learning disability requires special services (perhaps, as advocated by Sparks, Ganschow et al. [1992], a multi-sensory approach as opposed to a natural communication approach, for instance); in fact, what would most probably benefit students with foreign language difficulties is an "immersion in the culture of a country where the language is spoken" (Levine, 1987, p. 381). But, perhaps, it is also a matter of choosing the best time of readiness for some of these children.

I have tried as well to show that research in the field of second language learning is not sufficient to explain the learning difficulties of some students; our knowledge and understanding of the learning problems can benefit greatly from interdisciplinary research in fields which address human nature in all its diversity. Damasio (1994) is of the opinion that we really need greater knowledge about the "complex biological and socio-cultural machinery" of feelings so we can be "more aware of the pitfalls of scientific observation" (p. 246). Indeed, the domain of emotions is a very important one, as emotions are a key component of life and a vital source of energizing motivation; they give a sense of what is pedagogically feasible and possible, for learning cannot happen without emotional involvement. It is imperative then, that we listen and encourage every child to listen to the message the emotions transmit, for it is an existentially important message in which a call for a particular vocation often exists. Consequently, it can be said that emotions liberate and lead to constructive action.

I would like to emphasize that there is nothing wrong with students who cannot handle the Immersion program; a lack of motivation and poor attitude are not to be held responsible for the language learning differences of some of these students, but rather, we should see in those differences the reasons that affect the students' affective characteristics (Sparks & Ganschow, 1996). On one hand, it seems fair that every child should be afforded the opportunity of bilingualism, but on the other hand, it also seems unfair to make non-academically minded children persist in the learning of a subject for which they have no taste or aptitude. It may be unreasonable also to expect students with a weakness in phonology to be successful in a methodology that emphasizes listening and speaking as if the second language were to be acquired in the same manner as the native language (Sparks, Ganschow et al., 1992). Let us remember that the ultimate goal of education is to help in the development of the self and its potential and not to impose a situation which produces a "poorness of fit." So instead of insisting that children persist in a direction that brings much unhappiness, thwarts their educational progress and lowers their self-esteem, it is those particular skills that permit students to experience competence and self-efficacy which should be encouraged. After all, energies and effort invested into things should yield comparable results (Dinklage, 1991).

I sincerely wish and urge parents to discover who their children are. Children possess an inner voice and should be encouraged to listen to it and follow their own path in life, even if it does not correspond to their parents' expectations, aspirations or ambitions. Parents need to cultivate the flexibility which is required for total unconditional acceptance of their children's call in life; they owe it to their children to give them the opportunity to express their drives and talents in whatever form or career they choose, and to orient them to live with integrity. For this to happen, parents need to be understanding and receptive to their children's meaningful reality. However idealistic this may seem, parents need to develop a hermeneutic consciousness – a consciousness that helps them in relying on their own intuition and insight, and not those of others, in evaluating the learning situation or predicament of their children. Along the same conceptual line, Gardner (1993) is of the opinion that parents cannot arbitrarily decide what to bring up their children to do or to be; he advises the development of intelligences so children may be able to find their strengths and use them in a constructive way for the benefit of themselves and others:

> *In my view, the purpose of school should be to develop intelligences and to help people reach vocational and avocational goals that are appropriate to their particular spectrum of intelligences. People who are helped to do so, I believe, feel more engaged and competent, and therefore more inclined to serve society in a constructive way. (p. 9)*

A wrong education destroys vitality and leaves the mind a prey to destructive forces. A right education will produce human beings strong and sound in both body and mind. (Wilkinson, 1993, p. 36)

Notes

Introduction

1. In *The Essential Writings of Merleau-Ponty* (1969), Alden L. Fisher writes: "Phenomenology...does not expect to arrive at an understanding of man and the world from any starting point other than that of their 'facticity' (p. 27)....The real has to be described, not constructed or formed (p. 31)....To seek the essence of perception is to declare that perception is, not presumed true, but defined as access to truth (p. 38)....There is not a human word, not a gesture which has not some meaning" (p. 40).

2. Hermeneutics is primarily a philosophy of human understanding that aims at identifying the deeper meaning that underlies the surface meaning. Hermeneutic thought is diverse, but according to 20th century philosopher Gadamer, "The educated person is so 'dialogically sensitive' that the mere *presence* of the other [perhaps even to mind only] can break up her biases and enlarge her vision.... 'knowledge of human nature': this is the guiding ideal of contemporary social sciences in which one tries to 'discover typical behavior in one's fellowmen and can make predictions about others on the basis of experience'" (Blaker, D. [1993]. Education As The Normative Dimension Of Philosophical Hermeneutics. *Philosophy Of Education* [On-line], p. 4. Available: www.ed.uiuc.edu/EPS/PES-yearbook/93).

Chapter I

1. This name and all the other students' names used in this book are pseudonyms.

Chapter II

1. **Early Immersion**: students receive 100% of their instruction in French from Kindergarten until the end of Grade 2. Then, the proportion of instruction in French gradually decreases while the instruction in English gradually increases so that by the end of elementary school the two languages of instruction are balanced.

2. **Partial Immersion**: early- or late- provides half the curriculum in French and the other half in English.

3. **Late Immersion**: beginning in Grade 6, students receive 100% of their instruction in French; they continue in Grade 7 with 80% French instruction and 50% French instruction for the rest of their schooling.

4. See: "Cognitive and Attitudinal Consequences of Bilingual Schooling: The St. Lambert Project through Grade 6." *International Journal of Psycholinguistic Research, 5-6* (1976),p. 13.

    See also: Lambert, W.E., Tucker, G.R., D'Anglejan, A. (1973). "Cognitive and Attitudinal Consequences of Bilingual Schooling: The St. Lambert Project Through Grade Five." *Journal of Educational Psychology,* 65, pp. 141-159.

5. British Columbia Ministry of Education (Data Management and Student Certification Branch, April 1999, March 2000). *Headcount Enrolment in French Programs* [on line]. Available: www.bced.gov.bc.ca/k12datareports/

6. Bibeau bases his opinion on studies by Spilka, I.V. (1976): "Assessment of Second Language Performance in Immersion Programmes." *The Canadian Modern Language Review, 32*:5, 543-561; Connors, K. et al. (1977): *Evaluation of French Immersion Programme.* Baldwin-Cartier School Board Report. Montreal: Department of Linguistics, Universite de Montreal; Harley, B. (1984): "How Good Is Their French?" *Language and Society, 12,* 55-60.

7. Hammerly also bases his opinion on Spilka (1976). Adiv, E. (1980): "An Analysis of Second Language Performance in Two Types of Immersion Programs." *Bulletin of the Canadian Association of Applied Linguistics, 2*:2. 139-52. Tatto, M.A. (1983): *A Comparative Analysis of Grammatical Errors in the Written Code Between Grade Eleven Immersion French and Grade Eleven Core French.* (Unpublished Master of Arts – Teaching of French, Simon Fraser University). Pawley, C. (1985): "How Bilingual Are French Immersion Students?" *The Canadian Modern Language Review, 41,* 865-76. Hammerly also participated in the Pellerin and Hammerly Study (1986): "L'expression orale après treize ans d'immersion française." *The Canadian Modern Language Review. 42,* 592-606. In addition, he was a member of the committee that supervised a project by Rosanna Gustafson (1983): *A Comparison of Errors in the Spoken of Grades Two, Four and Six Pupils Enrolled in a French Immersion Program.* (Unpublished project, Master of Arts – Teaching of French, Simon Fraser University).

Chapter III

1. In 1991, the Lakehead Board of Education (Thunder Bay, Ontario) conducted a study of elementary students who had transferred from

Immersion to the English program because of difficulties. It was found that 12 of the 27 students rapidly progressed in English to average or above average marks. This seems to indicate that these students had academic difficulties specific to second language learning, not a learning disability per se.

Chapter IV

1. Studies concerning the achievement of minority language children were reviewed by Genesee (1976). He concludes: "The finding that the third language children scored as well as they did on some of the English tests is remarkable considering their lack of formal instruction in English. At the same time, their French language skills were comparable to the English based groups, despite differences in social class background....there is nothing in these data to suggest that French immersion would not be suitable for third language children" (p. 510). Romaine (1989) mentions that according to some studies, minority students born in Canada perform better in schools than students of English background. It is also this author's experience that children of minority language background succeed as well as majority language children in the Immersion program. In fact, they often surpass them.

2. Krashen, S.D. (1982). *Principles and Practice in Second Language Acquisition*. Oxford: Pergamon Press. Krashen posits four characteristics of optimal input for comprehension: 1. Optimal input is comprehensible, i.e. the message is understandable by the learner regardless of his/her level of second language proficiency; 2. Optimal input is interesting and/or relevant; 3. Optimal input is not grammatically sequenced; 4. Optimal input must be in sufficient quantity, although it is difficult to specify just how much is enough. (Cited by Cummins [1984] in *Bilingualism and Special Education*).

3. Wallace, G., Kaufman, J.M. (1981). *Teaching Children with Learning Problems*, 2nd edition. Columbus, OH: Charles E. Merrill.

4. Plata, M. (1982). *Assessment, Placement, and Programming of Bilingual Exceptional Pupils: A Practical Approach*. Reston, VA: The Council for Exceptional Children.

5. This excerpt from Plata (1982) is cited by Cummins (1984) in *Bilingualism and Special Education*.

6. Barnes, D. (1976). *From Communication to Curriculum*. Penguin.

7. The French immersion students were superior in their aural ability.

8. Later, Swain and Lapkin (1989) found from their observations of

Immersion classes that "overall, only nineteen percent of the grammatical errors made by the students were corrected, leaving eighty one percent ignored by the teachers" (p. 154). They then declared: "Learners not only need opportunities to produce the second language,...they also need to be 'pushed' toward a coherent, accurate, and appropriate production of their second language" (p. 154).

9. An interlanguage is an artificial language between native and foreign language produced by an interaction of the two language structures. Many researchers are of the opinion that when learning a second language, children actively organize the second language they hear along generalizations they make about its structures. Second-language errors are seen then as an attempt to test hypotheses about the structures of the second language and are thought to be similar to errors made by children acquiring their first language. However, other researchers feel the interlanguage reflects more of a negative transfer or mother tongue interference.

10. John Schofield: Interview. *Maclean's*, May 1, 2000.

Chapter V

1. The same year, Swain and Lapkin (1986) argued that grammar drills are not the answer to a better acquisition of language competence and that grammatical weaknesses in students' speech will be resolved through a high degree of language interaction.

2. Sparks, Ganschow et al. (1992) write that the foreign language (FL) "is learned in a 'multisensory' format [MSL], i.e. where students can 'hear', 'see' and 'do' [write] the language *simultaneously*....The rationale for a direct, MSL approach is derived from our recent empirical studies, the FL literature, and research on reading disabilities. In our empirical studies we have found significant differences in the phonological skills of successful and unsuccessful FL learners....An MSL approach is appealing for several reasons: [1] phonology and syntax are taught directly and explicitly in a systematic, step-by-step fashion; [2] a small amount of material is presented at one time; [3] material is thoroughly mastered before new material is introduced; and [4] a multisensory approach is used [Williams 1987]." *Annals of Dyslexia*, 42, 33-34.

3. Sweet, H. (1899). *The Practical Study of Languages*. Dent. Cited in P. Christophersen, (1973): *Second-Language Learning Myth and Reality*. Harmondsworth: Penguin Education.

4. Bi-directional collaboration between learner and different members of society.

5. Independent personal thinking.

6. Oxford and Shearin (1996) further explain that "the concept of scaffolding is directly linked to the idea of the zone of proximal development," defined as the distance between the learner's actual developmental level and the level of potential development (p. 137).

Chapter VI

1. Field independence is characterized by the ability and tendency to differentiate stimuli from a larger, integrating background of information, to separate the essential from the inessential and to be analytic.

   Field dependency is reflected in a sensitivity and attention to the background or surrounding information and a tendency to see the world as an unanalyzed whole.

2. Lesley Krueger is a journalist who specializes in education issues.

3. To that effect, Fillmore (1979) demonstrated very well how children of equal intellectual capacity differ in the ways they approach language learning and how cognitive and social factors of language acquisition interact together. She studied five young learners and found that the youngster that learned the least was the one who was not particularly interested in associating with speakers of the target language. The other youngsters socialized more and thus learned considerably more. Thus, the differences in the learning rates of the children had nothing to do with their cognitive capacity; it was mostly their social preferences that determined the outcome of the language learning process. And to explain the spectacular success of one of the five children studied, Fillmore says: "The secret…can be found in the special combination of interests, inclinations, skills, temperament needs and motivations that comprised her personality. It seems that she was inclined to do just those things that promote language acquisition" (p. 221).

4. Horwitz et al.'s source is: C.D. Spielberger: *Manual for the State – Trait Anxiety Inventory (Form Y)*. Palo Alto, CA: Consulting Psychologists Press, 1983.

5. Barr, V. (1993). *Foreign language requirements and students with learning disabilities*. (ERIC Digest No. 355 834). Washington, DC: ERIC Clearinghouse on Languages and Linguistics.

6. Levine, M.D. (1987). *Developmental variation and learning disorders* (p. 378). Cambridge, MA: Educators Publishing Service.

7. Wechsler Adult Intelligence Scale - Revised (WAIS-R, Wechsler, 1981).

8. "Linguists generally define phonology as the sound patterns of a language. Although the term used here also refers to sound patterns of a language, phonology is broadly defined as sound discrimination, the association of sounds with their written symbols, and the ability to phonetically divide words. Orthography refers to the 'visual representation of a language and can be defined as the written patterns of a language and their mapping onto phonology and meaning' [Aaron & Baker, 1991: p. 13]." in L. Ganschow, R. Sparks & E. Schneider, (1995, p. 77): "Learning a foreign language: Challenges for students with language learning difficulties." *Dyslexia: the Journal of the British Dyslexia Association, 1*, 75-95).

9. Ganschow, Sparks et al. (1995) mention that language learners vary from very good to very bad but that "a discrete entity such as a 'Foreign Language learning disability' implied in the 'deficit' notion does not exist" (p. 236). They later explain that "The change (from deficits to differences) was meant to reflect the notion of a continuum of difficulties with foreign language learning that ranges from mild to severe" (1998, p. 249).

10. Bouton (1974) mentions that some students' auditory problems impede their ability to concentrate. Also, some students suffer from a mild form of dyslexia that does not bother them until they start learning a foreign language (p. 226).

Chapter VII

1. The term "residue" used by Skehan (1989) was taken from J.B. Carroll (1973): "Implications of aptitude test research and psycholinguistic theory for foreign language teaching," in *International Journal of Psycholinguistics, 2* (5), 5-14.

2. Shore's references are: Hardy-Brown, K. (1983). "Universals and individual differences: Disentangling two approaches to the study of language acquisition." *Developmental Psychology, 19* (4), 610-624. Thompson, L.A. & Plomin, R. (1988). "The sequenced inventory of communication development: An adoption study of two- and three-year olds." *International Journal of Behavioral Development, 11* (2), 219-231. Munsinger, H. & Douglas, A. (1976). "The syntactic abilities of identical twins, fraternal twins, and their siblings." *Child Development, 47* (1), 40-50.

3. These authors also find that students with intact phonology but poor syntactic or semantic skills usually do not have FL learning problems until later (1996, p. 173).

4. "The modularity hypothesis maintains that some brain functions are

organized autonomously, and each uses special structures not shared by other systems. In Fodor's terms, the language processor is informationally encapsulated." (Sparks, R., Ganschow, L., Javorsky, J., et al., 1992, p. 414: "Identifying native language deficits in high-and low-risk foreign language learners in high school." *Foreign Language Annals, 25* (5), 403-417).

Carroll (1993) in *Human Cognitive Abilities* mentions that "The topic of neurobiological correlates of cognitive abilities is rife with speculation. Fodor (1983), for example, offers rationale and evidence for a theory that the brain is organized into independent 'modular' systems. Possibly some of these systems would correspond to broad factors of cognitive ability" (p. 661).

Pinker (199) in *The Language Instinct* also brings up the notion of module, "No one has ever studied heritable variation in language, but I have a strong suspicion of what it is like. I would expect the basic design of language, from X-bar syntax to phonological rules and vocabulary structure, to be uniform across the species....But the complexity of language circuitry leaves plenty of scope for quantitative variation to combine into unique linguistic profiles. Some module might be relatively stunted or hypertrophied. Some normally unconscious representation of sound or meaning or grammatical structure might be more accessible to the rest of the brain. Some connection between language circuitry and the intellect or emotions might be faster or slower" (p. 329).

5. Campbell (1992) mentions in his study of transfer students that 54% of the children do not enjoy hard work and only do enough work to get by. However, "it is impossible to state if more than half of the children leave the French Immersion program for these reasons" (p. 134).

Chapter VIII

1. Brad Evenson: Interview. *National Post*, May 1, 1999.

2. Kerry Gold: Interview. *The Vancouver Sun*, April, 4, 1998.

3. Elizabeth Grice: Interview. *The Vancouver Sun*, July, 18, 1998.

4. Sartre, J.P. (1964). *Words*. (Translated from the French by Bernard Frechtman). New York: George Braziller, Inc.

Chapter IX

1. Gardner (1993) refers to the linguistic and interpersonal intelligence as the *bio-psychological potential* (p. 37) that individuals (who differ for both

hereditary and environmental reasons) possess to deal with specific contents in the environment, such as the linguistic signals heard or produced, or the emotional information gleaned from interacting with other persons.

2. Gardner (1985) mentions that in the area of child development, there has been vigorous debate between the "holists, (like Piaget) who deem major intellectual functions to be the property of the brain as a whole" (p. 7), and the "localizers who believe that different portions of the nervous system mediate diverse intellectual capacities" (p. 7).

3. In *Educational Studies and Documents* (No. 37) published by UNESCO in 1978, David Elkind writes in the article titled: "Misunderstandings about how children learn": "What many parents fail to understand is that attempting to force young children to learn specific content may produce an aversion to academic learning in general. This distaste may have serious long-range effects on young children's academic achievement....A pernicious misunderstanding about young children is that they are most like adults in their thinking and least like us in their feelings. In fact, just the reverse is true, and children are most like us in their feelings and least like us in their thoughts....In large measure, all of these misunderstandings derive from a contemporary over-emphasis on intellectual growth to the exclusion of the personal-social side of development....I strongly believe that many problems in child rearing and education could be avoided if concern for children's achievement as students were balanced by an equally strong concern for their feelings of self-worth as people" (p. 50).

Conclusion

1. French Immersion Symposium (Ottawa, March 27, 1995). Dr. Fiedeorowiz has published extensively and received a number of awards, specifically the award for outstanding research given to her by the Council of Exceptional Children and another one by the International Reading Association for her outstanding contributions to learning disabled children and adults.

Bibliography

Adiv, E. (1979). *Survey of students switching out of Immersion and post-Immersion programs.* Province of Quebec: Protestant School Board of Greater Montreal.

Aljaafresh, A. & Lantolf, J.P. (1994). "Negative feedback as regulation and second language learning in the zone of proximal development." *Modern Language Journal, 78*, 465-483.

Averill, J.R. (1980). "Emotion and anxiety: Sociocultural, biological, and psychological determinants." In A. Rorty (Ed.), *Explaining emotions* (pp. 37-72). Los Angeles, CA: University of California Press.

Bandura, A. (1988). "Self-regulation of motivation and action through goal systems." In V. Hamilton, G.H. Bower & N.H. Frijda (Eds.), *Cognitive perspectives on emotion and motivation* (pp. 37-61). London: Kluwer Academic Publishers.

Barik, H.C. & Swain, M. (1976). "A longitudinal study of bilingual and cognitive development." *International Journal of Psychology, 2* (4), 251-263.

Barik, H.C. & Swain, M. (1978). "Evaluation of a French Immersion program: The Ottawa study through grade five." *Canadian Journal of Behavioral Science, 10*, 192-201.

Beitel, M. (1986). *Prognosis of learning disabled children in early total French Immersion programs.* Unpublished manuscript. Toronto, ON: York University.

Bernhard, J.K. (1993). "The effects of early French Immersion programs on the learning disabled: Two positions." *Exceptionality Education Canada, 3* (4), 1-18.

Bialystok, E. & Hakuta, K. (1994). *In other words: The science and psychology of second language acquisition.* New York: BasicBooks, Harper Collins Publishers.

Bibeau, G. (1984). "No easy road to bilingualism." *Langue et Societe, 12*, 44-47.

Bibeau, G. (1991). "L' apprentissage de la langue seconde: À quel moment l'entreprendre?" *Langue et Societe, 36*, 34-35.

Bibeau, G. (1991). "L'Immersion:…De la coupe aux lèvres." *Etudes de Linguistique Appliquée, 82*, 127-138.

Birbaumer, N. & Öhman, A. (1993). *The structure of emotion.* Toronto: Hogrefe & Huber.

Bogaards, P. (1991). *Aptitude et affectivité dans l'apprentissage des langues étrangères*. Paris, France: Les Editions Didier.

Bonyun, R., Morrison, F. & Unitt, J. (1986). *When primary pupils transfer out of Immersion*. Ottawa: Ottawa Board of Education, Research Centre.

Bouton, C.P. (1974). *L'Acquisition d'une langue étrangère*. Paris: Editions Klincksieck.

Bruck, M. (1978). "The suitability of early French Immersion programs for the language disabled child." *The Canadian Modern Language Review, 34* (1), 884-887.

Bruck, M. (1979). "Switching out of French Immersion." *Interchange, 9* (4), 86-94.

Bruck, M. (1982). "Language impaired children's performance in an additive bilingual education program." *Applied Psycholinguistics, 3* (1), 45-60.

Bruck, M. (1985). "Consequences of transfer out of early French Immersion programs." *Applied Psycholinguistics, 6*, 101-120.

Burns, G.E. & Olson, P. (1981). *Implementation and politics in French Immersion*. Toronto, ON: The Ontario Institute for Studies in Education.

Burstall, C. (1976). "Comments of guest analysts." (*Children with learning difficulties in primary French Immersion*: Trites, R.L.). *The Canadian Modern Language Review, 33* (2), 193-215.

Byrne, P. & Lester, L. (1983). "Psychoeducational correlates of central auditory processing dysfunction." In E.Z. Lasky, & J. Katz (Eds.), *Central auditory processing disorders* (pp. 331-342). Baltimore: University Park Press.

Calvé, P. (1983). "Commentary on the presentations of Dr. Morrison and Dr. Trites." In B. Kerr (Ed.), *Colloquium on French as a second language: Proceedings* (pp. 48-55). Toronto, ON: The Ministry of Education.

Calvé, P. (1986). "L'immersion au secondaire: bilan et perspectives." *Contact, 5* (3), 21-28.

Campbell, G. (1992). *Transferring from French Immersion: A case study of students who leave the French Immersion program upon completion of grade six*. Unpublished master's thesis, University of Manitoba, Winnipeg, Manitoba, Canada.

Carey, S. (1984). "Reflections on a decade of French Immersion." *The Canadian Modern Language Review, 41* (2), 246-259.

Carringer, D.C. (1974). "Creative thinking abilities of Mexican youth: The relationship of bilingualism." *Journal of Cross-Cultural Psychology, 5*, 492-504.

Carroll, J.B. (1976). "Comments of guest analysts" (R.L. Trites: *Children with learning difficulties in primary French Immersion*). *The Canadian Modern*

Language Review, 33 (2), 193-215.

Carroll, J.B. (1981). "Twenty-five years of research on foreign language aptitude." In K.C. Diller (Ed.), *Individual differences & universals in language learning aptitude* (pp. 83-118). Rowley, MA: Newbury House.

Carroll, J.B. (1993). *Human cognitive abilities.* Cambridge: Cambridge University Press.

Carroll, S. & Swain, M. (1993). "Explicit and implicit negative feedback: An empirical study of the learning of linguistic generalizations." *Studies in Second Language Acquisition, 15,* 357-386.

Cziko, G.E., Lambert, W.E. & Gutter, R. (1979). "French Immersion programmes and students' social attitudes: A multidimensional investigation." *Working Papers on Bilingualism, 19,* 13-28.

Child, N. (1989). "Should poor achievers transfer?" *Canadian Parents for French National Newsletter, 46* (5), 5.

Coquitlam School District. (1998). *Enrollment report.* Coquitlam, B.C.

Cummins, J. & Gulutsan, M. (1974). "Bilingual Education and Cognition." *Alberta Journal of Educational Research, 20* (3), 259-269.

Cummins, J. (1978). "The Cognitive development of children in Immersion programs." *The Canadian Modern Language Review, 34* (5), 855-883.

Cummins, J. (1979). "Should the child who is experiencing difficulties in early Immersion be switched to the regular English program?" *The Canadian Modern Language Review, 36,* 139-143.

Cummins, J. (1983). "Language proficiency, biliteracy and French immersion." *Canadian Journal of Education, 8* (2), 117-138.

Cummins, J. (1984). *Bilingualism and special education: Issues in assessment and pedagogy.* Clevedon, Great Britain: Multilingual Matters Ltd.

Cummins, J. & Swain, M. (1986). *Bilingualism in education.* London, Great Britain: Longman.

Damasio, A.R. (1994). *Descartes' error.* New York: G.P. Putnam's Sons.

Day, E.M., Shapson, S.M. & O'Shea, T.J. (1987). *General report: British Columbia French Immersion assessment.* B.C.: Ministry of Education.

Day, E.M. & Shapson, S.M. (1983). *Elementary French Immersion programs in British Columbia: A survey of administrators, teachers, and parents. Part II: Detailed Findings.* Burnaby, B.C. : University of Simon Fraser.

Deci, E.L., Ryan, R.M. & Willians, G.C. (1996). "Need satisfaction and the self-regulation of learning." *Learning and individual differences, 8* (3), 165-183.

Diaz, R.M. (1982). *The impact of second-language learning on the development of verbal and spatial abilities.* Yale University.

Dinklage, K.T. (1961). "Inability to learn a foreign language." In G.B. Blaine Jr. & C.C. McArthur (Eds.), *Emotional problems of the student* (pp. 185-206). New York: Appleton-Century-Crofts.

Dinklage, K.T. (1991). *Approaches to a student showing unusual difficulty learning a foreign language.* Paper given at The Kingsburg Center. Washington, D.C.

Dornyei, Z. (1994). "Understanding L2 motivation: On with the challenge!" *The Modern Language Journal, 78* (4), 515 -523.

Dube, S.L. (1993). *French Immersion withdrawal: Parental perspectives.* Unpublished master's thesis, University of Alberta, Edmonton, Canada.

Ehrman, M.E. (1996). *Understanding second language learning difficulties.* Thousand Oaks, CA: Sage Publications.

Ericsson, K.A. & Charnes, N. (1994). "Expert performance, its structure and acquisition." *The American Psychological Association, 49* (8), 725-746.

Eysenck, H.J. (1973). *The inequality of man.* London, Great Britain: Temple Smith.

Fillmore, L.W. (1979). "Individual differences in second language acquisition." In C.J. Fillmore, D. Kempler & W.S. Wang (Eds.), *Individual differences in language behavior* (pp. 203-228). San Francisco: Academic Press.

Gajar, A.H. (1987). "Foreign language learning disabilities: The identification of predictive and diagnostic variables." *Journal of Learning Disabilities, 20* (6), 327-330.

Gallimore, R. & Tharp, R. (1990). "Teaching mind in society: Teaching, schooling, and literate discourse." In I. Noll (Ed.), *Vygotsky and Education* (pp. 175-205). New York: Cambridge Press.

Ganschow, L., Sparks, R.L., Javorsky, J., Pohlman, J. & Bishop-Marbury, A. (1991). "Identifying native language difficulties among foreign language learners in college: A "foreign" language learning disability?" *Journal of Learning Disabilities, 24* (9), 530-540.

Ganschow, L., Sparks, R., Javorsky, J. & Patton, J. (1992). "Factors relating to learning a foreign language among high- and low-risk high school students and students with learnig disabilities." *Applied Language Learning, 3*, 37-63.

Ganschow, L. & Sparks, R. (1993). "'Foreign' language learning disabilities: Issues, research, and teaching implications." In S.A. Vogel & P.B. Adelman (Eds.), *Success for college students with learning disabilities* (pp. 283-320). New York: Springer-Verlag.

Ganschow, L., Sparks, R.L., Anderson, R., Javorsky, J., Skinner, S. & Patton, J. (1994). "Differences in language performance among high-, average-, and low-anxious college foreign language learners." *The Modern Language Journal, 78* (1), 41-54.

Ganschow, L., Sparks, R.L. & Javorsky, J. (1998). "Foreign language learning difficulties: An historical perspective." *Journal of Learning Disabilities, 31* (3), 248-257.

Gardner, H. (1985). *Frames of mind. The theory of multiple intelligences.* New York: Basic Books.

Gardner, H. & Hatch, T. (1989). "Multiple intelligences go to school. Educational implications of the theory of multiple intelligences." *American Educational Research Association, 18* (8), 4-10.

Gardner, H. (1993). *Multiple intelligences. The theory in practice.* New York: Basic Books.

Gardner, R. & Lambert, W.E. (1972). *Attitudes and motivation in second language learning.* Rowley, MA: Newbury House.

Genesee, F. (1976). "The suitability of Immersion programs for all children." *The Canadian Modern Language Review, 32,* 494-515.

Genesee, F. & Hamayan, E. (1980). "Individual differences in second language learning." *Applied Psycholinguistics, 1* (1), 95-110.

Genesee, F. (1983). "Bilingual education of majority language children: The Immersion experiments in review." *Applied Psycholinguistics, 4* (1),1-46.

Genesee, F., Holobow, N., Lambert, W.E., Cleghorn, A. & Walling, R. (1985). "The linguistic and academic development of english-speaking children in French schools: Grade 4 outcomes." *The Canadian Modern Language Review, 41* (4), 669-685.

Genesee, F. (1987). *Learning through two languages: Studies of immersion and bilingual education.* Cambridge, MA: Newbury House.

Genesee, F. (1992). "Second/foreign language Immersion and at-risk English-speaking children." *Foreign Language Annals, 25,* 199-213.

Goleman, D. (1995). *Emotional intelligence.* New York: Bantam Books.

Greenspan, P.S. (1980). "A case of mixed feelings: Ambivalence and the logic of emotion." In A. Rorty (Ed.), *Explaining emotions* (pp. 223-250). Los Angeles: University of California Press.

Greenspan, S.I. (1997). *The growth of the mind.* New York: Addison-Wesley.

Halpern, G., Martin, C. & Kirby, D.M. (1976). "Attrition rates in alternative primary school programs." *The Canadian Modern Language Review, 32* (5), 516-520.

Halsall, N.D. (1991). *Attrition/retention of students in French Immersion with particular emphasis on secondary school.* Ottawa: Canadian Parents for French.

Hamayan, E., Genese, F. & Tucker, R.G. (1977). "Affective factors and language exposure in second language learning." *Language Learning, 27* (2), 225-241.

Hammerly, H. (1988). "French Immersion (Does it work?) and the 'development of bilingual proficiency' report." *The Canadian Modern Language Review, 45* (3), 567-578.

Hammerly, H. (1989). *French Immersion: Myths and reality.* Calgary, Alberta: Detselig.

Harley, B. & Swain, M. (1978). "An analysis of the verb system used by young learners of French." *Interlanguage Studies Bulletin, 3* (1), 35-39.

Harley, B. (1984). "How good is their French?" *Language and Society, 12*, 55-60.

Hayden, R.H.M. (1988). "French Immersion drop-outs: Perspectives of parents, students and teachers." *Reading - Canada - Lecture, 6* (4), 222-229.

Heeson, J.A. (1982). *Individual differences in second language learning of Korean immigrant children.* Unpublished doctoral dissertation, University of Washington.

Hillman, J. (1996). *The soul's code.* New York: Random House.

Hoffman, M. (1983). "Psychological interventions for the child with central auditory processing disorder." In E.Z. Lasky & J. Katz (Eds.), *Central auditory disorders* (pp. 319-330). Baltimore: University Park Press.

Horwitz, E.K., Horwitz, M.B., Horwitz, M.B. & Cope, J. (1991). "Foreign language classroom anxiety." In E.K. Horwitz & D.J. Young, *Language anxiety* (pp. 27-36). Englewood Cliffs, NJ: Prentice Hall.

Jacobs, B. & Schumann, J. (1992). "Language acquisition and the neurosciences: Towards a more integrative perspective." *Applied Linguistics, 13* (3), 282-301.

Javorsky, J., Sparks, R.L. & Ganschow, L. (1992). "Perceptions of college students with and without specific learning disabilities about foreign language courses." *Learning Disabilities Research & Practice, 7*, 32-44.

Kagan, J. (1989). *Unstable ideas. Temperament, cognition, and self.* London, England: Harvard University Press.

Kagan, J. (1994). *Galen's prophecy. Temperament in human nature.* New York: Basic Books.

Kamin, J. (1890). *Difficulties in early French Immersion: A transfer study.*

Toronto, ON: The Ontario Institute for Studies in Education.

Keep, L.J. (1993). *French Immersion attrition: Implications for model building.* Unpublished doctoral dissertation, University of Alberta, Edmomton.

Keller, J.M. (1983). "Motivational design of instruction." In C.M. Reigeluth (Ed.), *Instructional design theories and models* (pp. 383-434). Hillsdale, NJ: Erlbaum.

Krashen, S.D. (1984). "Immersion: Why it works and what it has taught us." *Language and Society, 12,* 61-68.

Kuhl, J. & Kazen-Saad, M. (1988). "A motivational approach to volition: Activation and de-activation of memory representations related to uncompleted intentions." In V. Hamilton, G.H. Bower & N.H. Frijda (Eds.), *Cognitive perspectives on emotion and motivation* (pp. 63-85). London: Kluwer Academic Publishers.

Kuhl, P.K. & Meltzoff, A.N. (1997). "Evolution, nativism and learning in the developmnt of language and speech." In M. Gopnik (Ed.), *The inheritance and innateness of grammars* (pp. 7-44). New York: Oxford University Press.

Lanmark-Kaye, S. (1996). *The appeal of the early French Immersion program: A good match for gifted children?* Unpublished master's thesis, University of Simon Fraser, BC, Canada.

Lantolf, J.P. & Appel, G. (1994). *Vygotskian approaches to second language research.* Norwood, NJ: Ablex.

Lapkin, S., Swain, M. & Argue, V. (1983). *French Immersion: The trial balloon that flew.* Toronto, ON: The Ontario Institute for Studies in Education.

Lapkin, S. & Swain, M. (1984). "Research update." *Language and Society, 12,* 48-54.

Lapkin, S. & Carroll, S. (1988). "L'apprentissage du lexique français en classe d'immersion." *Quebec Français, 70,* 34-37.

Lapkin, S., Swain, M. & Shapson, S. (1990). "French Immersion research agenda for the 90s." *The Canadian Modern Language Review, 46* (4), 639-656.

Lasky, E. & Katz, J. (1983). *Central auditory processing disorders.* Baltimore: University Park Press.

Lebrun, M. (1988). "L'Immersion, une formule pédagogique à repréciser." *Québec Français, 70,* 32-33.

LeDoux, J. (1996). *The emotional brain.* New York: Simon & Schuster.

Lefebvre, R.C. (1984). "A psychological consultation program for learning-disabled adults." *Journal of College Student Personnel, 25* (4), 361-362.

Levine, M. (1990). *Keeping a head in school.* Cambridge, MA: Educators

Publishing.

Levine, M. (1987). *Developmental variation and learning disorders*. Toronto: Educators Publishing.

Lewis, C. & Shapson, S.M. (1989). "Secondary French Immersion: A study of students who leave the program." *The Canadian Modern Language Review, 45* (3), 539-548.

Lewis, C. (1986). *Secondary French Immersion: A comparison of those students who leave the program and those who stay*. Unpublished master's thesis, University of Simon Fraser, BC, Canada.

Lyster, R. (1987). "Speaking immersion." *The Canadian Modern Language Review, 43* (4), 701-716.

Mabbott, A.S. (1994). "An exploration of reading comprehension, oral reading errors, and written errors by subjects labeled learning disabled." *Foreign Language Annals, 27* (3), 293-316.

MacIntyre, R.B., Keeton, A. & Agard, R. (1980). *Identification of learning disabilities in Ontario*. Toronto, ON: Ministry of Education.

MacIntyre, P.D. (1995). "How does anxiety affect second language learning? A reply to Sparks and Ganschow." *The Modern Language Journal, 79* (1), 91-98.

MacIntyre, P.D. (1995). "On seeing the forest and the trees: A rejoinder to Sparks and Ganschow." *The Modern Language Journal, 79* (2), 245-248.

Macnamara, J. (1966). *Bilingualism and primary education*. Edinburgh: Edinburgh University Press.

Mandel, H.P. & Marcus, S.I., with L. Dean. (1995). *Why children underachieve and what to do about it*. Toronto: Harper Collins.

Moeller, P. (1988). "No, Sarah, early Immersion is not for you." *Venture Forth, 19* (3), 11-16.

Myklebust, H.R. (1994). *Understanding ourselves as adults*. Lake Worth, FL: Gardner Press.

Myer, B.J. & Ganschow, L. (1984). "Profiles of frustration: Second language learners with specific learning disabilities." In J.F. Lalande (Ed.), *Shaping the future of language education* (pp. 32-48). FLES, articulation and proficiency. Report of central states conference on the teaching of foreign language.

Nicolson, C.P. (1989). "Early French Immersion: Oui or non?" *Today's Parent*, February/March 1989, 31-34.

Norton, B. & Toohey, K. (in press). *Changing conceptions of good language learners: A window on SLA theory*.

Oller, J.W. (Jr.) (1981). "Research on the measurement of affective variables: Some remaining questions." In R.W. Andersen (Ed.), *New dimensions in second language acquisition research* (pp. 14-27). Rowley, MA: Newbury House.

Olson, P. & Burns, G. (1983). "Politics, class, and happenstance: French Immersion in a Canandian context." *Interchange, 14* (1), 1-16.

Oxford, R.L. & Shearin, J. (1996). "Language learning motivation in a new key." In R. Oxford (Ed.), *Language learning motivation: Pathways to the new century* (pp. 121-144). University of Hawai'i at Manoa.

Parkin, M., Morrison, F. & Watkin, G. (1987). *French Immersion research relevant to decisions in Ontario.* Toronto, ON: Ministry of Education.

Pawley, C. (1985). "How bilingual are French Immersion students?" *The Canadian Modern Language Review, 41* (5), 865-876.

Peal, E. & Lambert, W.E. (1962). "The relation of bilingualism to intelligence." *Psychological Monographs, 76,* 1-23.

Pimsleur, P., Sundland, D.M. & McIntyre, R. (1964). "Under-achievement in foreign language learning." *International Review of Applied Linguistics in Language Teaching, 2* (2), 113-139.

Pinker, S. (1994). *The language instinct.* New York: W. Morrow.

Pinter, R. & Keller, R. (1922). "Intelligence tests for foreign children." *Journal of Educational Psychology, 13,* 214-222.

Pompian, N.W. (1986). "Like a Volvo lifted off my chest." *The Undergraduate Bulletin, 5* (3), 1-2.

Poth, J. (1980). *National languages and teacher training in Africa* (No. 32). Paris, France: Unesco.

Poth, J. (1988). *National languages and teacher training in Africa.* (No. 47). Paris, France: Unesco.

Ratey, J.J. & Johnson, C. (1997). *Shadow syndromes.* New York: Pantheon Books.

Rivers, W. (1976). "Comments of guest analysts." (*Children with learning difficulties in primary French Immersion*: Trites, R.L.). *The Canadian Modern Language Review, 33* (2), 193-215.

Romaine, S. (1989). *Bilingualism.* Oxford, U.K.: Blackwell.

Rorty, A. (1980). *Explaining emotions.* Los Angeles: University of California Press.

Saer, O.J. (1923). "The effect of bilingualism on intelligence." *British Journal of Psychology, 14,* 25-28.

Schumann, J.H. (1994). "Where is cognition? Emotion and cognition in second language acquisition." *Studies in Second Language acquisition, 16* (2), 231-242.

Schwarz, R.L. & Lavine, R.Z. (1996). *Principles for teaching learning disabled foreign language learners.* American University.

Scovel, T. (1978). "The effect of affect on foreign language learning: A review of the anxiety research." *Language Learning, 28* (1), 129-141.

Service, E. (1992). "Phonology, working memory, and foreign-language learning." *The Quarterly Journal of Experimental Psychology, 45A* (1), 21-50.

Shapson, S.M. (1985). "Post-secondary bilingual education: Identifying and adapting to the shift in second language demands." *The Canadian Modern Language Review, 41* (5), 827-834.

Shore, C.M. (1995). *Individual differences in language development.* Thousand Oaks: Sage Publications.

Skehan, P. (1989). *Individual differences in second-language learning.* London, Great Britain: Athenaeum Press.

Skehan, P. (1991). "Individual differences in second language learning." *Studies in Second Language Learning, 13* (2), 275-298.

Skutnabb-Kangas, T. & Toukomaa, P. (1976). *Teaching migrant children mother tongue and learning the language of the host country in the context of the socio-cultural situation of the migrant family.* Helsinki: The Finnish National Commission for UNESCO.

Sparks, R.L., Ganschow, L., Javorsky, J., Pohlman, J. & Patton, J. (1992). "Identifying native language deficits in high- and low-risk foreign language learners in high school." *Foreign Language Annals, 25* (5), 403-416.

Sparks, R.L., Ganschow, L., Pohlman, J., Skinner, S. & Artzer, M. (1992). "The effects of multisensory structured language instruction on native language and foreign language aptitude skills of at-risk high school foreign language learners." *Annals of Dyslexia, 42,* 25-53.

Sparks, R.L. & Ganschow, L. (1993). "Searching for the cognitive locus of foreign language learning difficulties: Linking first and second language learning." *The Modern Language Journal, 77* (3), 289-298.

Sparks, R.L., Ganschow, L. & Patton, J. (1995). "Prediction of performance in first-year foreign language courses: Connections between native and foreign language learning." *Journal of Educational Psychology, 87* (4), 638-655.

Sparks, R.L. & Ganschow, L. (1996). "Teachers' perceptions of students' foreign language academic skills and affective characterisics." *Journal of Educational Research, 89* (3), 172-185.

Spilka, I.V. (1976). "Assessment of second-language performance in Immersion programs." *The Canadian Modern Language Review, 32* (5), 543-561.

Steiner, R. (1966). *Study of man.* (D. Harwood, Trans.) London: Rudolf Steiner Press. (Original work published 1919)

Stern, H.H., Swain, M. & McLean, L.D. (1976). *French programs – some major issues.* Toronto, ON: Ministry of Education.

Stern, H.H. (1984). "A quiet language revolution: Second-language teaching in Canadian contexts – Achievements and new directions." *The Canadian Modern Language Review, 40* (5), 506-524.

Stern, H.H. (1982). "French core programs across Canada: How can we improve them?" *The Canadian Modern Language Review, 39* (1), 34-47.

Stern, M. (1991). *The French Immersion transfer process: Investigation of children transferring from the French Immersion program into the regular English program.* Unpublished doctoral dissertation, University of Toronto, Ontario, Canada.

Swain, M. & Lapkin, S. (1982). *Evaluating bilingual education: A Canadian case study.* Clevedon, Avon: Multilingual Matters.

Swain, M. & Lapkin, S. (1986). "Immersion French in secondary schools: 'The goods' and 'the bads'." *Contact, 5* (3), 2-9.

Swain, M. & Lapkin, S. (1989). "Canadian Immersion and adult second language teaching: What's the connection?" *The Modern Language Journal, 73* (2), 150-159.

Tatto, M.A. (1983). *A comparative analysis of grammatical errors in the written code between Grade eleven Immersion French and Grade eleven core French.* Unpublished master's thesis, BC, Canada: University of Simon Fraser.

Thomas, A. & Chess, S. (1984). "Genesis and evolution of behavioral disorders: From infancy to early adult life." *The American Journal of Psychiatry, 141* (1),1-9.

Toates, F.M. (1988). "Motivation and motion from a biological perspective." In V. Hamilton, G.H. Bower & N.H. Frijda (Eds.), *Cognitive perspectives on emotion and motivation.* London: Kluwer Academic Publishers.

Tremblay, P.F. & Gardner, R.C. (1995). "Expanding the motivation construct in language learning." *The Modern Language Journal, 79* (4), 504-520.

Trites, R.L. & Price, M.A. (1976). *Learning disabilities found in association with French Immersion programming.* Toronto, ON: Ministry of Education.

Trites, R.L. & Price, M.A. (1977-1979). *Assessment of readiness for primary French Immersion.* Toronto,ON: Ministry of Education.

Trites, R. & Moretti, P. (1986). *Assessment of readiness for primary French Immersion*. Ontario: Ministry of Education.

UNESCO. (1953). *The use of vernacular languages in education*. Paris, France: Unesco

UNESCO. (1991). *World education report*. (United Nations Educational Scientific and Cultural Organization). Dijon, France: Darentière.

Van Els, T., Bongaerts, T., Extra, G., Van Os, C. & Janssen-van Dieten, A. (1984). *Applied linguistics and the learning and teaching of foreign languages*. Baltimore, MD: Edward Arnold.

Vedovi, C.L. (1992). *Raisons des parents, des instituteurs et des orthopédagogues relatives au transfert des élèves du programme d'immersion française au programme anglais*. Unpublished master's thesis, BC, Canada: University of Simon Fraser.

Waterston, C. (1990). *Switching out of French Immersion in London, Ontario, 1988-89*. Unpublished master's thesis, University of McGill, Québec, Canada .

Webster, P. (1986). "Secondary Immersion: Parent expectations & reality." *Contact, 5* (3), 10-13.

Weininger, O. (1982). "Learning a second language: The Immersion experience and the whole child." *Interchange, 13* (2), 20-40.

Wilkinson, R. (1993). *Rudolf Steiner on education*. Stroud, Gloucestershire, U.K.: Hawthorn Press.

Williams, M. & Burden, R.L. (1997). *Psychology for language teachers: A social constructivist approach*. U.K.: Cambridge University Press.

Wiss, C.A. (1989). "Early French Immersion programs may not be suitable for every child." *The Canadian Modern Language Review, 45* (3), 517-529.